Alfred W. Tatum

READING
for their
LIFE

(Re)
Building the Textual Lineages
of African American Adolescent Males

HEINEMANN
Portsmouth, NH

Foreword by
Michael W. Smith

Heinemann
361 Hanover Street
Portsmouth, NH 03801–3912
www.heinemann.com

Offices and agents throughout the world

Credits continue on page xix.

Library of Congress Cataloging-in-Publication Data
Tatum, Alfred W.
    Reading for their life : (re)building the textual lineages of African American adolescent males / Alfred W. Tatum ; foreword by Michael W. Smith.
        p. cm.
    Includes bibliographical references and index.
    ISBN-13: 978-0-325-02679-4
    ISBN-10: 0-325-02679-3
    1. African American boys—Education (Secondary).   2. Teenagers with social disabilities—Education (Secondary)—United States.   3. Reading (Secondary)—Social aspects—United States.   4. African American boys—Books and reading.   5. African American teenagers—Books and reading.   6. African American boys—Race identity.   I. Title.
    LC2779.T37 2009
    428.0071'2—dc22   2009021877

Editor: Lisa Luedeke
Production editor: Patricia Adams
Typesetter: House of Equations, Inc.
Cover design: Lisa Fowler
Interior design: Jenny Jensen Greenleaf
Manufacturing: Steve Bernier

Printed in the United States of America on acid-free paper
13 12 11   VP   2 3 4 5

Dedication

To Educators who work tirelessly to promote reading and writing
to our nation's adolescents

To the students of the Chicago Public Schools

Contents

Foreword

"Twenty-first-century America has no clear and consistent remedy for educating its darkest sons." So says Alfred Tatum—and the data he presents makes that proposition unarguable. Even those (Mead 2006) who question the significance of boys generally underperforming girls in literacy have to see that 'crisis' is not too strong a word to use when discussing the literacy achievement of African American young men, especially those from working-class and working-poor families.

Tatum begins his book by explaining the scope of the problem and the racial isolation and social dislocation that contribute to it. But if you know Alfred Tatum you know that he has no patience for excuses. In fact, despite the bleak statistics that he shares, I think this book is profoundly optimistic.

In the first place, this book is profoundly optimistic about the power of literature to transform lives. Tatum shares some of the texts that helped make him who he is today and he thinks hard about the qualities of those enabling texts that promise to occupy an important place in the textual lineages of the African American adolescents with whom he works. Literature isn't a matter of cultural literacy for Tatum; as his subtitle indicates, it's a matter of life and death. As Tatum explains, reading and writing literature can be the vehicle for contemplating such crucial questions as "What are you willing to sacrifice to create the life you want to live?" and "How does one recover a part of one's soul?" Tatum makes a compelling case for the historic importance of "brother and sister" authors of various races, times, and places to African Americans grappling with forces that are working to keep them down. He also makes a compelling case that schools are denying current students a chance to experience the importance of literature in their own lives through a focus on contentless skills and the use of texts that are irrelevant or watered-down. Not only does Tatum share texts that he has read, he also shares stories and poems that he has written that get at the heart of the issues important to kids he encounters.

The book is also profoundly optimistic about African American young men. The writing of his summer workshop students is truly powerful.

> Yet here I stand
> With success and failure in each hand
> Will I falter in my ways letting time go [by] like sand
> But I tell myself NO . . .
> Everything is possible with the right tools in your hand.

Tatum warns against oversimplifying and underestimating. To those who say that these young men reject reading, Tatum asks how can they reject something that [they] have not fully experienced? Instead of following this conventional wisdom, he documents their engagement in texts that matter.

Finally, Tatum is profoundly optimistic about teachers. Although he argues that educators must courageously accept that we are part of a social and educational system that contributes to the underperformance of African American adolescent males, he believes that we have the power to change that sad fact: "It is my hope that through this book, other teachers will find a way to squeeze texts for every ounce of possibility they contain to advance the literacy development of African American adolescent males." He points the way not only by sharing his ideas about enabling texts, but also by sharing his ideas about enabling instruction. He details how to use essential questions to motivate and reward students' reading. He explains how to use the text to teach the text. He explains how to use students' reading in service of their writing and vice versa. In short, we have the power to make a difference. All we need is the will.

This book is a call to action. I hope we heed its cry.

—Michael W. Smith

References:
Mead, S. 2006. The Truth About Boys and Girls. *Education Sector.* *http://www.educationsector.org/usr_doc/ESO_BoysAndGirls.pdf*

Acknowledgments

I believe writing is a personal act imbued by emotions. It is inevitable that there will be shifts in one's emotions as he/she writes any text of considerable length. I experienced multiple emotional shifts while writing *Reading for Their Life,* over the past two years. These shifts occurred as I read autobiographical and biographical accounts by and about African American males that discussed their relationships with texts. My emotions were rocked as I read newspaper accounts of the lives of young citizens being snuffed out by gun violence, namely in Chicago and other large urban areas. The summer of 2008 was exhilarating as I hosted the first African American Adolescent Male Summer Literacy Institute at the University of Illinois at Chicago, allowing me the opportunity to support the literacy development of young African American males aspiring to become writers. Then, my own writing about adolescent males, as the father of an adolescent male middle schooler, created a new level of anxiety that I had never experienced as a writer.

Through all the emotional shifts, and as I struggled to place the right words on the page with the right tone, Lisa Luedeke, was a steadfast supporter of this project. Her patience with me throughout the process and her presence at multiple speaking engagements where I toyed with the ideas found in this text were invaluable. It has been an extremely positive experience to have my writing embraced by the Heinemann family.

I would also like to acknowledge my older son, Amal-Sundar Tatum, who managed to endure my insistence that he read certain texts and evaluate if they made the cut to become a part of his textual lineage. He became the home-based arbiter of my writing. I was equally encouraged by my younger son, Andrew Tatum, who sleeps with several books each night. He continually reminds me of the hope and promise found in texts even for the youngest among us.

Then, there are the young men who shared their writings and lives with me over a five-week period during a summer institute. There was power in their words and power in their presence. They pushed me in ways that are hard to capture in writing, but I am a better person after having shared the same space with these young African American males. I am thankful to all the supporters of the summer institute.

Finally, I would like to acknowledge my best friend and wife, Sabrina Tatum, who is the key to all my professional and personal undertakings. Without her, the work is not possible. Her comments, support, and commitment to the same ideals of providing quality texts and a meaningful education to young folks throughout the United States allow me to keep my emotions in tact and writing on track. I am eternally grateful.

—Alfred W. Tatum
Chicago, Illinois

Introduction

We need to be honest about the literacy development of African American adolescent males in the United States. African American males are a distinct part of the fabric of American schooling—not more outstanding, but shelled differently. There are more than four million African American males enrolled in grades K–12 in the United States, making them seven percent of the school-aged population. Like all adolescents, they have multiple, overlapping identities. It would be pretentious of me to claim that I can adequately capture the complexity of African American adolescent males. That is not the goal of this text.

But it is impossible to deny the problems and tensions many of these young males face. There are clear indicators that their literacies in both reading and writing remain underdeveloped. Countless anecdotes reveal that many, especially those attending chronically underperforming schools, have not reconciled how they "fit" in compulsory educational contexts.

This is a critical juncture in our history. Many young people of color in economically underdeveloped communities are becoming deeply rooted in personal and academic dormancy that interrupts their ability to invest in our fast-moving, ever-changing, increasingly demanding world. It is becoming more and more difficult to function and prosper in culturally isolated urban ghettos, desolate rural areas, and first-ring suburbs—all places whose demographics are shifting as a result of widespread community destabilization.

These communities and circumstances of turmoil have prompted one African American male in his early forties to propose the following solution:

> Dig a hole large enough for ten million of these young men, advertise free government-Link cards to attract them and some of their parents to the hole, and put a lid on the hole before setting it on fire.

This proposed genocide, offered in what we want to assume is ironic hyperbole, should nevertheless stop us in our tracks. How have we gone so terribly wrong? One hundred years ago, the challenge in improving the lives of African American youth was identifying the best form of education—which was viewed as the key to their social, economic, political, and spiritual advancement. That sense of promise has mutated into vitriolic despair and despondency. For many African American adolescent males today, the seeds of intergenerational poverty and social dysfunction continue to be watered.

In this text, I propose an alternative that is within our control, not out of naïveté or disillusionment, but on the basis of clear thinking informed by historical precedence and bodies of research that have advanced our thinking of what it means to provide high-quality literacy education. My proposal is grounded in hope for the improved futures that reading and writing provide.

Neither effective reading strategies nor literacy reform will close the reading achievement gap or life outcome gap unless meaningful texts are at the core of the curriculum and educators know how to mediate such texts. We need to carefully critique the texts we require African American adolescent males to read as well as how these texts are positioned in the curriculum and taught in our classrooms. Based on our examination of how their school experiences are shaped—not only by how well they read but also by *what* they read—we need to help African American adolescent males develop the language and competence to understand, explain, and respond to various school and life situations. Teachers and administrators must embrace these broader aims in order to advance the literacy development of these young men and to do the work necessary to be able to teach and collaborate with them.

Educational practices for African American adolescent males living in high-poverty communities or economically disadvantaged homes in middle-income communities must have the interdisciplinary depth, theoretical grounding, and attention to responsive pedagogy necessary to address their needs within and among the many contexts in which their lives are being shaped: poverty, violence, premature sexual activity, fatherless households, negative gang influences, limited religious influences, and community destabilization.

All too often, African American adolescent males do not receive an education that helps them define and shape a positive existence within the world in which they find themselves. They lack sufficient exposure to texts that they find meaningful and that will help them critique, understand, and move beyond some of the turmoil-related experiences they encounter outside school. This *underexposure to texts* shapes reading, writing, language, and vocabulary achievement gaps and contributes to a life in which young African American males as a group experience greater economic, judicial, and social strife and disappointment.

Many school administrators and teachers experience feelings of *learned powerlessness* when asked to provide high-quality instruction to African American adolescent males struggling to navigate school and their tenuous life experiences. I have been asked:

1. Is it possible to teach young adolescents without having lived the African American male experience in America?

2. Is it reasonable to expect African American boys in high-poverty schools or from economically disadvantaged homes to perform as well as other students academically?

3. Do we have to separate African American boys from other students in order to educate them?

These educators are admitting that they find it difficult to teach African American adolescent males living in poverty.

Among the reasons for this are:

1. They do not fully understand the continually shifting African American male experience in the United States or what it means to be entrenched in turmoil-producing conditions.

2. They do not understand or accept historical forces and the residual effects of race-based slavery and the intentional demasculinization of African American males.

3. They do not understand or accept the effects of current stifling educational policy mandates and the destabilization of many urban and rural centers.

4. They are unaware of educational practices that have been effective with African American males.

It has been argued that we need to recruit more African American male teachers. This is the focus of programs like Call Me Mister ("Mister" is the acronym for Mentors Instructing Students Toward Effective Role models), which was launched at Clemson University in South Carolina when statistics indicated that a dismal one percent of South Carolina's more than twenty thousand teachers were African American men. Momentum is also developing to open all-male middle and high schools for African American boys in large cities such as Chicago and New York. The success of such initiatives ultimately depends on how we respond to these challenges in all our schools.

The challenge for *all* educators in advancing the literacy development of African American adolescent males converges around the same issues. Will their literacy instruction translate into observable literacy behavior such as increased reading and writing of texts both in and outside school, improved vocabulary, language acuity and facility, feelings of self-efficacy on reading and writing tasks, improved outcomes on formal and informal reading and writing assessments, and significant increases in high school graduation rates in the short term? In the long term, will their instruction yield observable evidence that African American males are thinking differently about their lives, enrolling in institutions of higher education at greater rates, and becoming key players in larger numbers in an increasingly diverse world as a result of the literacy instruction they were provided in schools?

The purpose of this book is to provide a broader understanding of using texts with African American adolescent males as part of a larger goal to shift the paradigm for educating these young males. Texts connected to larger academic, cultural, economic, political, social, and personal aims help these young males define who they are and what they can become; help them become resilient; and move them to engage positively with others for their own benefit and that of the larger society.

The idea of using reading and writing as meaningful and significant tools for living precedes my lifetime. I am the beneficiary of others who have accepted this principle and writers who have penned texts that have seeped into my soul and stretched my humanity over the years. I merely wish to remind educators of the power texts harbor for adolescents and how texts are laden with possibilities for counteracting the aimless wandering, discontent, sadness, hopelessness, despair, and unhealthy psyches impaired by turmoil-induced or other restrictive conditions.

This book is about *building the textual lineages* of African American males by (re)connecting them to texts that are *useful* and texts that *matter to them*. A textual lineage, similar to lineages in genealogical studies, is made up of texts (both literary and nonliterary) that are instrumental in one's human development because of the meaning and significance one has garnered from them. For example, Dick Gregory's autobiographical account, *Nigger*, is part of my textual lineage because it released me from the stigma of poverty, causing me to think differently about my life and moving me to read other texts that strengthened my resolve to remain steadfast as I negotiated a community of turmoil—the Chicago housing projects—in the 1970s and 1980s. Gregory's text changed my life. (A longer discussion of textual lineages is undertaken in Chapter 4.)

Although I am convinced that *all* students benefit from reading meaningful and significant texts and having the opportunity to create such texts, I pay particular attention to the young African American adolescent males who need our concentrated attention to reshape their literate lives—the ones mothers are referring to when they ask me, "What can I do to help my son out?" or "How can I help my son who has a lot of potential but is having a hard time succeeding in school?" or "Can you please give me *something* I can do to help my son? I just don't know what to do." These are legitimate pleas, wrapped in parents' love, for us to safeguard the lives and futures of their sons.

If we indeed are to safeguard a quality education for African American adolescent males, we need to address several fundamental misconceptions.

First, we must get rid of the notion that African American boys do not want to be educated.

That many educators have a difficult time believing this is evident in such instructional practices as exposing these young boys to fewer texts or requiring them to read texts that have nothing to do with empowering them or helping them navigate school and society. Differentiated instruction or age-old curricular traditions are used to legitimize this practice. Without careful analysis of the critical issues facing these young men, it is difficult to provide responsive instruction, whatever name we attach to it.

These young men experience unquantifiable pain when they struggle with reading. Yet they often mask their pain (to their disadvantage) to protect their identity in what they perceive as hostile, uncaring environments shaped by uncommitted educators. A young high school student who participated in a focus-group discussion I led told me, "If I didn't have a mentor outside of North East High School I would probably drop out. It's scary not knowing how to read. I don't want to be in school anymore. I am tired of being made fun of." Clearly, limited reading skills caused this young man internal anguish.

The pain many of these young men experience may cause them to state openly, as one did in a documentary about Douglass High School in Baltimore, "Fuck academics, that's for them nerdy motherfuckers. I am going to keep it gutter." Providing explicit skill and strategy instruction alone cannot interrupt this type of thinking. There is something deeper at work here. We have to think deeply to counter a mindset that causes one to embrace the notion, "I am going to keep it gutter." The gutter, in all its connotations, has been shattered before as readers have been put into "immediate confrontation with [their] wounded minds" (Morrison 2004, xvi). Texts, mediated in powerful ways, can interrupt ill-informed thinking.

Second, we must get rid of the notion that African American adolescent males should accept any form of instruction.

In many cases, they have legitimate reasons to resist instructional practices that will leave them underprepared in society. They know when instruction is a lie. I observed such a lesson in a freshman high school reading classroom near the end of the academic year. The students, predominantly African American males, were asked to identify misspelled words in a sentence written on the board. One of the misspelled words was *laff* (*laugh*). This lesson, extrapolated from an elementary school orientation of reading instruction, did not provide a cognitive challenge and was not developmentally appropriate for high school students. In the same high school I observed a teacher telling the students which letters to capitalize while completing a worksheet on the capitalization of proper nouns, a lesson that lasted for more than thirty minutes. Neither lesson brought these students any closer to becoming better readers or writers. Students will reject the texts and the education they are being offered if they determine that both lack significance and meaning.

Third, we must get rid of the notion that adolescents need saviors before they need quality education.

They need human- and text-based literacy models. Quality education allows African American male adolescents to shape their identities and become self-invested. Quality teaching and quality texts matter. Teachers have the power to help shape the lives of African American adolescent males and move them beyond some of the limitations that impede their literacy development. However, many African American boys feel loathed before they are loved, feel rejected before they are respected, and feel alienated before they are educated. These feelings often morph into expressions of anger.

African American boys who have feelings of anger or who feel a lack of psychosocial membership in the classroom often perform poorly in school

(Price 2000; Spencer 1999) and may become hostile—a hostility that often leads to disproportionate disciplinary actions.

African American boys continue to underperform in school as they *wait for educators to get it right*. We must ask ourselves:

1. Are we ready for them?

2. Do we have what they need when they enter our schools and classrooms?

3. Are we being truly thoughtful and reflective in our practices?

Time to reshape the life trajectories of many of these young males through literacy development is running out earlier and earlier as they opt for deleterious pathways that recycle and cement failure.

As I think about the welfare and literacy development of African American adolescent males, I am challenged by the following questions:

1. How are we conceptualizing literacy instruction for them?

2. How are we teaching these boys to read and write, and what texts are we using?

3. How do policies, mandates, curriculums, and personal beliefs affect teachers who are genuinely concerned with addressing the literacy needs of these young men?

4. How are we nurturing the *identities* of these young men?

5. How are we supporting these young male's belief in themselves as academic, cultural, economic, human, social, and spiritual beings?

6. How are we helping these young men enjoy school?

In essence, the penetrating question—"What is U.S. 'schooling' doing *to* or *for* African American adolescent males?"—led me to write this book for people, in whatever educational system (middle and high schools, community colleges or university-based reading courses, social services organizations, and juvenile justice institutions) who are directly responsible for educating African American adolescent males. Each of these groups will benefit from a discussion of text-based variables that are being underemphasized and creating disharmony in the literacy education of African American males.

Educators need to reexamine their relationships with African American males, young males who will benefit from expressed affection, caring, and a disciplined resolve. Too often these young men have their smiles, their childhood, their silliness, and their humanity neglected as they are viewed as *at-risk*, as *delinquent*, and as *behavior problems*. As a result they are rendered invisible or adopt a psyche of invisibility.

Although the focus of this book is on African American adolescent males, I am in no way undermining the significance of addressing the literacy needs of other adolescents in crisis. As I have written elsewhere:

> A false polarization is often evoked when efforts are aimed to specifically address the literacy needs of African American adolescent males. It is often intimated that a concentrated focus on African American males suggests that the literacy needs of . . . other adolescents are less important or do not require the same attention. This is simply not the case. It is the case, however, that literacy reform efforts and approaches used to improve the reading achievement and life outcomes of African American adolescent males are woefully inadequate and suffer from an underestimation of the depths of their literacy needs in largely racially segregated schools and racially integrated schools. (Tatum 2008, 156)

African American males in U.S. schools have a small margin for error. As the young adult novelist Sharon Flake writes in *Bang* (2005), "A black boy don't get a hundred chances to get it right. Sometimes, he just gets one. That's it. . . . You blow your chance, you blow your life" (124). One poor grade too many, one discipline problem too many, one outburst too many, may lead to the capricious misconduct of assigning special labels to these young men—thus typically initiating their removal from regular education classrooms. We must find ways to *get with* African American adolescent males in schools as opposed to *getting on* them.

How This Book Is Organized

The book is divided into two parts.

Part 1—which comprises Chapters 1, 2, and 3—focuses on the urgency of building textual lineages. In the first chapter, I discuss how African American males growing up in the 1990s and the first decade of the twenty-first century have been and continue to be impacted by public policy, popular culture, and communities of turmoil in which a fear of violence is paramount. (Can you imagine what it feels like to go to school in a city in which more than thirty students were murdered in one academic year? That's what happened in the Chicago Public Schools during 2007–2008 and 2008–2009.) In Chapter 2, I situate African American male adolescents within the nation's literacy crisis. This historical orientation has present-day implications for engaging young African American males in literacy as a collaborative act. In Chapter 3, I describe four vital signs of literacy development that call attention to four parallel gaps that affect achievement.

Part 2, which comprises Chapters 4–8, focuses on texts and how they can be used to pay attention to various contexts—international/national, community, economic, cultural/social/gender, and personal—that lead African American adolescents to become engaged with texts in schools and other educational contexts. I make the argument that building the textual lineages of African American adolescent males is critical to advancing their literacy development. This focus places their lives in a larger context that expands beyond and requires a rethinking of the school context.

Each chapter is anchored by one or two "essential questions" (Beach et al. 2006; Smith and Wilhem 2006) that should be considered by educators, students, or both as part of this rethinking effort. The idea of literacy development as a mechanism for change guides this text.

PART I:
THE URGENT NEED TO BUILD
TEXTUAL LINEAGES

African American Adolescent Males

■ **Essential question for educators and students:** How do I become and remain resilient?

> Look at me and know to destroy me is to destroy yourself.... We are not so far apart as it might seem.... It is our common search for a better life, a better world.... I too am America. America is me. It gave me the only life I know—so I must share in its survival. Look at me. Listen to me.... There is yet a chance for us to live in peace beneath these restless skies.
>
> —GORDON PARKS

Late one evening driving through one of Chicago's inner-city communities with visible signs of social and economic suffering, I counted more than sixty young men occupying the sidewalks and porches in a two-mile stretch. They appeared to range in age from ten to mid-twenties. Later I was reminded of Liebow's 1967 study of the Negro street-corner men, written more than forty years ago. He described a shifting collection of anchorless adults who came together in a run-down section of Washington, D.C. during the 1960s. The street-corner men were characterized as losers who were not going anywhere and were painfully aware of that reality. They moved about in a kind of indeterminate state because of a lack of education and skills.

Liebow provided a striking account of the aspirations of young men who felt trapped on the street corners because of their circumstances and limited academic preparation. One of the men, Richard, offered these comments:

I graduated from high school but I don't know anything. I'm dumb. Most of the time I don't even say I graduated, 'cause then somebody asks me a question and I can't answer it, and they think I was lying about graduating. . . . They graduated me but I didn't know anything. I had lousy grades but I guess they wanted to get rid of me. (55)

Liebow explained how many an African American man living in that inner-city environment adopted an attitude of hopelessness about his future. He writes, "It is a future in which everything is uncertain except the ultimate destruction of his hopes and the eventual realization of his fears" (66). Still,

The desire to be a person in his own right, to be noticed by the world he lives in, is shared by each of the men on the street corner. Whether they articulate the desire or not, one can see them position themselves to catch the attention of their fellows in much the same way as plants bend or stretch to catch sunlight. (61)

Poverty Default

Approximately twenty-five percent of the total African American population in the United States lives below the poverty line. However, many African American families reside in extreme poverty tract communities in which over fifty percent of the residents live below the poverty line (Wilson 1996). There is a "poverty default" in these communities—a higher degree of racial segregation from the larger society, inadequate health care, degraded school life in classrooms with a predominant African American population, neighborhoods plagued by lower levels of social organization, rates of violent criminal behavior exceeding those of other neighborhoods, a substantial number of adults who are unemployed or who have dropped out of the labor force altogether, a high number of births out of wedlock and births to teen parents, and institutionalization associated with drug use and other illicit activities.

Poverty bites. One parent in a poor community explained her nervous breakdown this way: "I was going crazy in my head, trying to figure out how to get my kids out, to protect them. . . . I knew [living in this community] was going to grind them down" (Anson 1987, 67). She was afraid that her sons would become trapped in the Harlem ghetto in which they lived. Her fears were realized when one of her sons was murdered by a New York police officer shortly after he won a scholarship to Stanford University.

Parents are concerned about the safety and welfare of their sons. I received the following email in June of 2006:

Hello, Mr. Tatum,

My name is [Concerned Mother]. I know you will be speaking in Philadelphia at a conference this week. I know this letter probably won't reach you by the time you come here. I have a son who is 16 years old. . . . I have tried everything to reach him and it feels like I'm losing him slowly but surely. I, along with his grandparents have raised [Son]. . . . The School District of Philadelphia assisted me in putting [Son] into a very good school. He now goes to [Urban School], a school for children with disciplinary problems. He spends a lot of his time with friends smoking marijuana and I'm afraid. Can you please assist me in a letter of encouragement to him that everyone makes bad choices sometimes? He doesn't have to continue his life on the road to destruction.

Several months earlier I had become involved in the life of another sixteen-year-old, who participated in a research study I conducted. A relative of this young man was concerned about her African American teenage son. She feared he would be dead or in jail in three years if he did not become a better reader. She feared her son would drop out of school and carve out a criminal path. (At the time of this writing, the son has dropped out of school as the mother feared.) This mother connected her son's projected criminality or death with reading ability since he was retained three times in the Chicago Public Schools because he failed to achieve a prescribed minimum standard on the district's reading assessment.

Relying on Schools

What does it mean to have to rely on schooling if you are an African American adolescent male living in extreme poverty in one of America's tract communities? Frankly, it's a crapshoot. The dilemma this presents is evident in schools throughout the United States. The impact of poverty and poverty-related conditions on academic achievement is clearly revealed in educational statistics. On average, twenty-six percent of U.S. eighth graders are reading at or above a proficient level according to the National Assessment of Education Progress (United States Department of Education 2007). This disheartening percentage is significantly lower in areas with a large number of public school students. For example, only twelve percent of the eighth graders in Washington, D.C. are reading at or above a proficient level, compared with thirty-seven percent of the students in Maine and New Hampshire—states with significantly fewer students.

African American boys, though unaware of these statistics, are living them. My conversation with an African American sixteen-year-old after he read the speech Bill Cosby delivered in commemoration of the fiftieth anniversary of *Brown vs. Board of Education* illustrates this point. Cosby mentions that more than 50 percent of African American males drop out of high school. Quincy, who was not going to school at the time, said, "I realized that Bill Cosby was talking about me." I asked him if he had been aware of the dismal statistic before reading the speech. He responded:

> No. I haven't even heard about that. The most I ever heard about the blackfolk population in school is when we're doing Martin Luther King, Malcolm X, Rosa Parks, the first lady astronaut [Dr. Mae Jemison, the first African American woman to travel into space], and all those people that we are familiar with. If we can learn about the first lady astronaut we can learn about this other stuff. I see a lot of young African American men hanging out, but I did not know the statistic was that high.

Exiled in America

Twenty-first-century America has no clear and consistent remedy for educating its darkest sons—African American adolescent males—and not nearly enough serious, systematic efforts are being made to address the literacy of these young males. The full truth is that many African American males are exiles on American soil. Some even want to quit America, but there is nowhere for them to go. Randall Robinson (2004), after encountering a group of young African American males on his way to a speaking engagement in Rochester, New York—young men moving in and out of a damaged bus shelter, going nowhere on a sunny school-day afternoon—describes them as a single entity:

> Now he is a menace to society. He knows this but not how he became this. He really doesn't give a fuck either. He knows his name but not who

he is. He simply cannot remember. His memory was stolen from him. Not his memory of cultural contemporary fact but his memory of a cultural traditional to which he, before it, once belonged in a long stream of time. Even if he knew he had lost something or had something taken from him, he would have a thought of measure of himself. As it was, he thought nothing of himself because he was, he concluded, nothing. (21)

As an African American male born at the end of the 1960s, I embraced schooling as the hope for my future and had teachers who, without reservation, held the same hope for me. However, I had friends who lived above and across the street from me in Chicago's Ida B. Wells housing projects who did not appear to embrace school as the hope for their future. Some were more aligned with Randall's description above. They began to cut school. They began to smoke weed. They began to gangbang. Some even began to kill. Two different members of my eighth-grade graduating class placed me at gunpoint; one was a member of my little league baseball team. Both were later incarcerated for long periods of time.

Racial Isolation and Social Dislocation

This chapter does not attempt to define authentic blackness, the essence of which has been the subject of debates and tension in the African American community (Akbar 1991; Dyson 2004; McWhorter 2003). Nor will I attempt to provide an authentic notion of what it means to be a man, since I don't want to become trapped by narrow ideas about "masculinity." I also resist the temptation to describe the African American adolescent male as a victim.

What I am doing in this chapter is calling attention to how risk factors related to an African American adolescent male's existence (e.g., poverty, poor schooling, negative community contexts, poor self-efficacy) add to his vulnerability, how notions of being African American and male impact young men living in poor communities, and how these young men shape their existence. I describe this through the lens of a literacy educator interested in reconnecting these young men with texts primarily *in school*, but also in other contexts. I have learned that we must know how to thrust reading and writing upon them when they appear before us, and I have observed the positive impact and improved academic outcomes when we get it right (Tatum 2000, 2003, 2006a).

I am particularly concerned with African American adolescent males who view their community circumstances in situationally adaptive ways (Wilson 1996)—those who

1. perceive that severe restrictions have been imposed on them by a hostile environment;

2. have difficulty sustaining motivation;

3. have no ideological counterweight to challenge the ideology they shape for themselves;

4. underperform academically and experience years of failure in schools and society.

Very few educators, social workers, community members, and policy makers have figured out ways to advance the literacy of these young males on a large scale that yields positive measurable impacts on reading and writing assessments.

African American Males Born in the 1990s

Sociologists note that in the 1990s parents, educators, and students in poor communities began to experience a low sense of collective efficacy, a feeling of inability to take the steps necessary to achieve desired goals. It has become a triple threat—parents, educators, and students (the critical tripartite)

1. get tired of trying,

2. give up,

3. and become despondent and pessimistic about their ability to succeed.

Many African American parents give up after getting tired of trying to improve the reading and writing of their adolescent sons who struggle academically. It becomes overwhelming. Below are the reflections of two adults living on the South Side of Chicago about the feelings of low self-efficacy engendered by their own failure to ensure the welfare of their children. The first comment is from a twenty-eight-year-old unmarried mother of two who lives in a large housing project. The second is from a thirty-five-year-old mother of three who lives in a poor neighborhood.

Because, like I said, to get discouraged, if—I don't care how far you are down the road, to get discouraged takes you back halfway. Because then you got to get your self-esteem up again, you know you have to get the motor goin' again. And that's what I feel is the biggest downfall for people in the neighborhood. They just give up. (Wilson 1996, 77)

Sometimes you can try and then you say "I'm tired of trying." I have did that. You try so hard it seems as if when you just about to get up, something happen to knock you back down and you just forget it, then. 'Cause I did that many a time. (Wilson 1996, 77)

The late 1980s and the 1990s saw an economic reversal that catapulted many communities into a downturn. Around the same time the growth of drug use and an increase in other illicit activities in heavily populated neighborhoods further debilitated these communities. The late 1980s also brought the explosion of a new genre of music, West Coast hip-hop, which ushered in mind-shaping gangster rhymes and the carrot provided by the commercial success of rap personalities. Arguably, those who felt a personal connection to the music more readily accepted the lyrics. As violence escalated in communities across the nation, a debate about the impact of this music on the "moral health of America's young" began (Watkins 2005). Gruesome acts of violence took place in many urban and rural communities heavily populated with African American and Latino males.

An administrator told me about an incident that took place while I was working as a consultant in a Washington, D.C. high school. A young man was shot in the back of the head and then propped up in the center of the athletic bleachers with a hood over his head. His body was discovered when students arrived the next morning. In *Monster: Autobiography of an L.A. Gang Member*, Sanyika Shakur (1993) describes the contemplation and execution of another violent incident:

We plotted and planned most of the night trying to decide on which act [of violence] would most grab the [rival gang's] attention. We pondered castration, blinding, sticking a shotgun up the victim's rectum and pulling the trigger, and cutting off his ears. . . . Combing the streets of the Sixties 'hood in a desperate attempt to find one of their shooters, the crew drove block after block, stopping civilians to ask the whereabouts . . . of their elite crew of shooters. Finding none of them around, they settled for an up-and-coming Ghetto Star. They seized him, beat him into submission, and chopped off both his arms at the elbow with machetes. One arm was taken, and the one arm was discarded down the street. (72–73)

Incidents of violence similar to the ones described above led to the criminalization of African American and Latino males.

Political ideologies related to youth crimes also shifted in the 1980s and 1990s. During these years, California became the state with the nation's largest prison population and corrections system because of sweeping changes in the juvenile justice system. California Proposition 21 (Prop 21) increased a variety of criminal penalties for crimes committed by youths and incorporated many youth offenders into the adult criminal justice system. The philosophy that juvenile justice systems held toward rehabilitation came under attack as media images of juvenile crime became more graphic. Politicians gained political capital by becoming tough on youth crime and espousing tougher crime laws that garnered the support of older, more well-to-do voters. The image of the African American and Latino male became one of the young superpredator, a new species of criminal.

There were more than one million prisoners in U.S. state and federal prisons in 1994, a tripling of the prison population in 1980. The prison population surpassed the two million mark by the middle of 2002. According to the statistics of the Bureau of Justice, more than twelve percent of all African American males from twenty-five to twenty-nine years old were in prison at the end of 2002, compared with two percent of Latino males and one percent of white males in the same age range. The 1980s and 1990s were characterized as the "punishment decade," as prison culture became dominated by African American males with a disadvantaged background. Changes in legal statutes, such as Prop 21, singled out young people for being who they are. Watkins (2005) writes, "The triple bind of race, class, and youth made life a real challenge. . . . To be young . . . and poor was almost a crime itself during the punishment decade" (179).

Music Hath More Than Charms to Soothe

In hip-hop music, African American males are self-proclaimed prophets who use lyrics full of inspiration or tragedy (Perry 2004). Volleying between inspiration and tragedy, these young males are left dangling between America's promise and America's wilderness. Asante (2003) discusses the promise and the wilderness as social and political metaphors in American society. The promise implies that something good is to be expected. The wilderness implies something difficult, perhaps unknown—a place where one does not know what to expect. This view is captured in the following lyrics by two hip-hop artists, one widely recognized and the other living in relative obscurity:

> *I really need to talk to you, Lord. Since the last time we talked, the walk has been hard. I know you haven't left me, but I feel like I'm alone. I am a big boy now, but I'm still not grown.*
> —*DMX, "Lord Give Me a Sign"*

◆ ◆ ◆ ◆ ◆

> *I grew up in the streets of Roxbury where too many brothers were being buried under rocks. . . . Life was like a real life boot camp living in Boston twenty-four seven. So believe me when I tell you Beantown was more than what you see coming out of Harvard and MIT.*
> —*Omekongo Dibinga, "My Life Is a Reality Show"*

These lyrics reflect the wilderness and promise experience in different ways. DMX's promise is the hope of receiving instructions from the Lord to help him survive the hard walk of the wilderness that causes him to feel alone as he seeks manhood. For Omekongo, who describes his life as a reality show, the wilderness is Roxbury, Massachusetts—where brothers are dying because of cocaine so close to the promise of Harvard and MIT.

The image of dangling between the wilderness and the promise was made painfully real to me during a visit to Urban Prep Charter Academy for Young Men, an all-male African American high school on Chicago's South Side. After spending a morning walking the halls and listening to administrators discuss the success stories of the young males attending the school and looking at the college banners that decorated the halls, I later observed an African American teenager being arrested by a detective within a few feet of the school. The excitement I felt in the school was tempered by seeing this young man in a wristlock that controlled his movement. The expressionless teenage boy's hopeless stance countered the promise inside the school where young men wearing blazers and ties (and referred to as "little Obamas" by the school's founder) move from classroom to classroom. The wilderness I often observe outside schools is partly shaped by economic deprivation that causes some African American adolescent males to see everything as meaningless, worthless, and lifeless.

Hip-hop music became a widespread outlet for African American males in the 1990s. It expresses rage and intimates expressions of psychological pain. It also treats the criminal underworld and interpersonal conflicts as mere dysfunctions (Perry 2004). It became possible for a hip-hop artist to become rich expressing that rage in the 1990s. More important, it gave African American males a new way to think about and express themselves. Russell Simmons, a hip-hop mogul, explains the intersection of social structure and hip-hop this way:

> When I was sixteen, I wanted to be an entrepreneur, but selling weed was one of the few options open to me. Today, however, young people now have all these people visible who make the choice to be entrepreneurs and inspire them to do the same. It's now a cultural thing in our community. Being a teacher, maybe a doctor, these used to be hopes and aspirations of our community. But now hip hop is all they talk about. Lower-middle-class boys in New York City were the absolute dumbest kids you could find anywhere, same as you would find in the projects down the block. Well, it's the same dumb people who broke the mold, because they were so hip hop and so angry and so fuck this. I'm going to make it on my own. It's like, own a company. (Gates 2004, 52)

A Generational Shift

"Where once the means to freedom was thought to be literacy or reclaiming the principles of the Declaration of Independence or utilizing the legal system—or taking up guns—for hip-hop entrepreneurs, the means, according to Simmons, is hardheaded capitalism, and the goal, massive profits" (Gates 2004, 6). Collins (2006) offers:

> Coming to adulthood after the decline of the Civil Rights and Black Power movements of the 1950s and 1960s, contemporary youth grew up during a period of initial promise, profound change, and, for far too many, heart-wrenching disappointment. During this period marked by the end of the Black Power movement and the ascendancy of hip hop, they lived the shift from color-conscious racism that relied on strict racial segregation to

a seemingly colorblind racism that promised equal opportunities yet provided no lasting avenues for advancement. (3)

The young entrepreneur became the new urban revolutionary in the 1990s and beyond. Revolution is no longer about marching for civil rights, it is about getting paid.

Literacy instruction has to respond to this generational shift and occur in a context in which African American adolescent males see that they matter. They want to be acknowledged. The following is from an interview I conducted with a male sixteen-year-old in 2005:

TATUM: What is your purpose for living?

YOUNG MALE: To be an African American.

TATUM: What does that mean to you?

YOUNG MALE: It's saying like half the black population is in jail or dead. I want to be the one who is trying to make something out of myself. Try to get a name out there. Basically, try to make a living.

TATUM: Why is it important for you to say African American?

YOUNG MALE: Because that's what I am, African American. That is basically what I am trying to do, be somebody so people can see what African Americans can do.

His identity as an African American was important to this young male because he felt he was the devalued other. He believed others viewed his identity as negative. Patricia Collins, in *From Black Power to Hip Hop* (2006), would describe this young male as part of a "generation whose actual members remain written off, marginalized, and largely invisible in everyday life" (3). She adds:

Isolated and ghettoized within American society, "domestic" youth—namely, those who are neither foreign migrants nor the children of migrants from countries of the Caribbean, continental Africa, or Europe—represent a highly stigmatized yet important population. (3)

During the same interview the young male shared that "African Americans need to show people what we can do." When I asked what people, he said:

Basically anybody and everybody. African Americans need to show the population that we can make something out of ourselves. We don't need to be the only ones on the streets and stuff. We need to be out on a job. For instance, some people can be president, us, African Americans, the majority of the world ain't going to let that happen because they don't think we are worthy enough to take control and handle what we need to do. [He made this statement before Barack Obama's successful presidential run.]

Later in the conversation he suggested that teachers do not know how to handle students:

TATUM: You said something interesting. You said teachers do not know how to handle kids, some of them might be scared. Talk about that a little more.

YOUNG MALE: 'Cause they think we are worthless. They think we are just going to give up. We won't do what we need to right. They try to help us but they won't help us constantly get back on track.

The Bridge to Opportunities

The devaluing or dismissing of economically poor African American adolescent males in school and society; public policy that has commodified them as superpredators; economic social structures that reduce the collective self-efficacy of these young men and those charged with protecting their welfare; and the influence of hip-hop culture and its music on their thinking has made it increasingly challenging for teachers to address the literacy of these young men in today's schools. Education does not have a strong gravitational pull for many of these young males, particularly in environments that do not acknowledge their identities. This leaves them trapped in poor communities, unaware of the wide range of possibilities available to them and without the literacy tools to carve out these opportunities.

Engaging these young males in reading and writing texts that pay attention to their multiple identities—academic, cultural, economic, gendered, personal, and social—becomes a bridge to opportunities. Texts must be used effectively to honor and nurture the multiple identities of these young men. If not, many of them will remain in economically oppressive conditions—and the reading, writing, language, and vocabulary achievement gaps that send these young males to the back of the line will persist. They will continue to lack the language and knowledge to create their own texts—a generation without a recorded voice to increase their opportunities for social engagement, uplift, and intellectual development. The following poem captures these sentiments:

The Failure Dance
by Alfred Tatum

It is common knowledge among many African American adolescent males
    that teachers use us as training grounds.
Although your intentions are good, we know that you do not want to be
    around us for long.
You will cut out when a better teaching opportunity presents itself. (I would
    too!)
We sit in the classroom squandering and acting out with substitute after
    substitute as you continue to collect your paychecks.
This is not hidden from our eyes.
We experience your abandonment as we abandon ourselves.
We know what you say when you go home and talk about those black
    boys in those schools.
We hear the voices of your spouse and parents who tell you that you need
    to get out as soon as possible.
They do not understand why you put up with that lost generation (or
    whatever names they call us).
We know this.
We are not lost. We are right here, but you fail to see us. We hardly see
    ourselves.
You have to prove yourself to us before we give you the chance.
Maybe it should not be this way, but we lack the emotional maturity to act
    otherwise.
You are not teaching me anything anyway with your skill and drill sheets
    that require little thought to plan.
You simply make copies, pass the sheets along, and voice how I need to be
    serious about my future.

continues

You are banking on those pages to help shape my future while you are
    planning a way to abandon me for your own future—your own inner
    sanity. How can I take you seriously when you do not take yourself
    seriously?
But, we got each other so I guess we will continue the *failure dance* until
    the new administration comes.
You will escape or leave and we will remain trapped.
Good luck at your next interview when you share your inner-city teaching
    experience with the hiring team at your new school.
They will be impressed, while we remain oppressed.
We are *all* guilty.

Understanding more about African American adolescent males does not in itself lead to better literacy teaching. Although it is essential to center their literacy development around their identities, their experiences, and the issues critical to their development, we need to know *how* to use these identities, experiences, and issues to provide high-quality strategy and skill instruction that doesn't leave these young males behind. We must not overlook the humanity of these young males and their need for human development. We need to shape literacy as a collaborative act in our schools and classrooms.

Shaping Literacy as a Collaborative Act

■ **Essential question for students:** How can literacy be used as a tool for engagement?

■ **Essential question for educators:** What are the appropriate pathways for human development? Who and what needs to be involved?

So, I didn't spring fully formed out of some racial Zeus's head; I was shaped and molded in an environment where achievement was taken for granted, where excellence was expected, where aspiration was crucial, and where intellectual engagement was the norm of the day—on every level.

—MICHAEL ERIC DYSON

That single moment of triumph pushed me to want to read more. From then on, it was as though I could not read enough books.... I had not been content to read and to learn. I also felt I had to let everyone else in the world know how brilliant I had become.

—BEN CARSON

Historically, African American reading and writing were collaborative acts involving a wide range of texts that held social, economic, personal, political, or spiritual significance. For example, Negro literary societies (also known as reading-room and debating societies) were formed in nine states and the District of Columbia in the late 1800s. The societies were often gender-specific. One of the more popular societies often chronicled as part of this history is the Young Men's Literary and Moral Reform

Society of Pittsburgh and Vicinity. Others included the Gilbert Lyceum, in Philadelphia; the Phoenix Society, in New York City and Baltimore; the Young Men's Literary Society, in Boston; and the Young Men's Lyceum and Debating Society, in Detroit.

Book talks in these societies were referred to as "mental feasts" (Wesley 1939), talks that profoundly affected the young men. After reading the works of black authors like Frederick Douglass, a male participant in one of these societies wrote that he realized that "these limbs were never meant to be chained in servitude" (Lilien 2001). *The Liberator*, an antislavery pamphlet edited by William Lloyd Garrison, was a common topic of discussion in reading-room societies. These societies had a wide range of purposes, including:

- building up a collection of useful books on every subject for the benefit of their members,

- enlightening the group by means of weekly lectures on literary and scientific subjects,

- preparing their members to participate in public platforms,

- promoting the improvement of colored people in moral conduct, literature, and the mechanical arts,

- training youth in the habits of reading and reflection,

- cultivating the mind and improving the heart, and

- strengthening intellectual faculties and cultivating refined literary taste.

These purposes are clear examples of early curriculum theorizing based on the existing circumstances of African Americans, namely to improve their lives. Noticeably absent are the halting iterations that govern today's literacy practices in schools throughout the United States (e.g., minimum standards, adequate yearly progress). Several of the earliest societies were active for a decade or more before dissolving. Literary societies expanded to more states in the second half of the nineteenth century and continued through the early part of the twentieth before losing steam.

Literacy was also a collaborative part of African American males' meaningful and purposeful activism. For example, African American "conductors" operated the nineteenth century's Underground Railroad and carried out other antislavery and resistance activities using various forms of oral, written, and graphic communication. African American newspaper agents traveled to large cities and remote areas to distribute their materials.

Many African American Civil War troops also benefited from collaborative literacy events. "Although they engaged in combat and performed some of the most difficult work associated with the war, African American soldiers also took time to become literate. Whenever they had a spare moment, out would come a spelling-book or primer or Testament, and you would often see a group of heads around one book" (Williams 2005, 50). Below, a man describes stumbling on a camp of black troops:

> Going up a light rise where stood several large tents, I stopped, and was cordially invited to enter. There were four or five in the great tent, and to my great surprise some were reading, and others writing. All were neatly dressed and looked nice in their uniforms. During the day the chaplain taught the men; at night they studied together. The sight of the black men reading so impressed [the man's eleven-year-old companion] that he soon got hold of a Webster's blue-back reader and began taking lessons from a member of his regiment. (51)

African Americans have walked along somewhat different paths toward literacy (Belt-Beyan 2004). One constant was being regularly and purposefully engaged with print within a meaningful, social context. Describing the acquisition of literacy by a young boy, Belt-Beyan writes:

> Neither Martin's inner desire to read nor his struggle to acquire the tools of literacy were sufficient in themselves to make him a real reader in his own eyes, but it was the slave community that made him realize that he was indeed a reader. He became a confident, able reader for being regularly and purposefully engaged with print within a meaningful social context. Specifically, he received recognition and encouragement for his endeavors from significant people in his life who listened, praised, and observed his progress. . . . Thus reading and writing events were collaborative acts. (102)

Collaborative literacy events were among the many informal ways the African American community promoted literacy. Have we lost this? Can this communal approach be reconstructed in today's schools or other educational settings?

Shaping literacy development through collaboration can be effective with African American adolescent males because "people are produced by cultures and communities, by larger networks of association, love, kin, affection, and so on" (Dyson 2004). In the epigraph at the beginning of this chapter, Dyson explains how he was shaped and molded in an environment in which achievement was taken for granted. He goes on to say, "It wasn't done so much by teachers deploying . . . a pedagogy geared toward instilling pride, but as they took for granted that folk could achieve and love each other. . . . They gave us a sense of helping ourselves without harming others" (5).

As we become more knowledgeable about culturally responsive approaches to literacy teaching (Gay 2000; Schmidt and Ma 2006; Tatum 2005), which emphasize caring, commitment, culpability, and competence (and value cooperation over competition), we potentially move closer to shaping literacy as a collaborative act. Here are several things we can do to bring this about among and with African American adolescent males.

1. *Show we care.* Let African American adolescent males know we care about them by challenging them and paying attention to their voices and concerns. Caring is essential to their literacy development—and to their becoming actively involved in that development. Becoming a better teacher of African American boys begins by inviting their voices into the process (Tatum 2000, 2006b).

2. *Reflect before we reject.* Like all adolescents, African American adolescent males display signs of adolescent immaturity. However, we tend to react more quickly and more strongly to their immature behavior. One young man told me, "Teachers are quick to send you out for a quick descent to the principal's office to get suspended or something when all they have to do is talk to us."

3. *Aim wide.* We need to take a broader view of literacy development. Literacy instruction is more than "just teaching students how to read and write" (see Figure 2.1). It is being responsive to students' many needs and shaping a trajectory that leads to positive life outcomes (see Figure 2.2). When reading collides with some form of race-based, class-based, or language-based disadvantage, students are learning amid turmoil. This turmoil cannot be ignored or treated as a limitation.

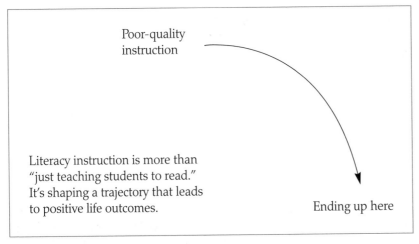

Poor-quality
instruction

Literacy instruction is more than
"just teaching students to read."
It's shaping a trajectory that leads
to positive life outcomes.

Ending up here

Fig. 2.1: *Negative Outcome of Literacy Instruction*

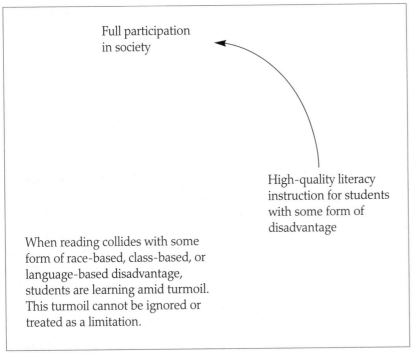

Full participation
in society

High-quality literacy
instruction for students
with some form of
disadvantage

When reading collides with some
form of race-based, class-based, or
language-based disadvantage,
students are learning amid turmoil.
This turmoil cannot be ignored or
treated as a limitation.

Fig. 2.2: *Positive Outcome of Literacy Instruction*

Wearing Books Out Together

James Baldwin said, "The first book I read through was *Uncle Tom's Cabin*. I read it so many times I nearly wore it out." African American males wear books out that they find meaningful and useful. I cannot recall how many times I have read the *Souls of Black Folks*; *The Autobiography of Malcolm X*; *Invisible Man*; *Black Boy*; *Why We Can't Wait*; *Black Skin, White Masks*; *Visions for Black Men*; and *The Fire Next Time*. (I first encountered several of these texts during my middle school and high school years.) Each time, I discover something new that escaped me during my previous readings.

Following the Annual Conference of the National Association of Black School Educators held in November 2007, I received the following email from an African American gentleman who attended a professional development seminar during which I discussed how African American males revisit texts they find meaningful without being prompted:

> Good Morning, Dr. Tatum,
>
> Thank you so much for sharing your work on teaching African American boys. I too am concerned about the plight of our young men in our nation's classrooms today. I thought it was profound when you had all the books that impacted you as a student in your presentation. It gave me joy to know that there were only two books I did not read. [It is worth noting that this man and I read many of the same books although we were from different regions of the country.] As for *The Learning Tree* by Gordon Parks, *I must have read that book six times* [my emphasis]. I later bought my own copy as an adult.

The wearing out of texts, as reflected in numerous autobiographical accounts, was most evident during the Afrocentric movement of the 1960s and 1970s. During this time, African American males read and passed along texts as they sought ways to fight against the Man/PIG/White Honky—as they strove for consciousness in the American contexts of race, class, and power. In 1966, for example, the Black Panthers set down twenty-six rules for members of the party. Rule 23 stated, "Everyone in a leadership position must read no less than two hours per day to keep abreast of the changing political situation" (Foner 1970, 6). The most recent introduction to *Negroes with Guns* (Williams 1998) states that this text became one of most significant influences on the Black Panther Party for Self-Defense, headquartered in Oakland, California.

When I invited one of my colleagues, who attended college in the mid-1970s, to describe the role of texts in his life, he shared how he and his African American male friends "wore out" *They Came Before Columbus* (Van Sertima 1976). They coordinated the book's return and immediate re–check out from the university library, which imposed a four-week limit, and they met in a dorm room or some other location to discuss the book. "We passed the book among ourselves until it literally became worn out." They had created what I refer to as a "purposeful literacy cooperative." Purposeful literacy cooperatives are a viable structure for advancing African American males' reading and writing inside and outside schools.

Wearing books out was not unique to African American men in educational settings. Eldridge Cleaver, who wrote the memoir *Soul on Ice* (1968), tells how he "devoured [*Negroes with Guns* by Robert Williams] and let a few friends read it, before the [prison] library dug it and put it on the list" (71) of books to which prisoners were denied access. I can only imagine the consternation the following paragraph stirred among prison guards:

> I am not afraid of alienating white friends of our liberation movement. If they really believe in the liberation movement they will not resent deviation from the old worn path that has led us in this fruitless circle. . . . They speak of tolerance, but they display unlimited intolerance toward those Afro-Americans who refuse to become their puppets and yes-man Uncle Toms. (34)

Cleaver characterizes these passed-along texts as "books that one wants to read—so bad that it [causes] a taste [in] the mouth" that must be satisfied (70).

Books like these nourish people as they try to function in the society and time in which they live; they ultimately become part of one's textual lineage. As educators, we need to help (re)connect African American boys to texts that provide guidance and road maps for *being, doing, thinking,* and *acting.*

Brother and Sister Authors

The authors of these literary and nonliterary passed-along texts became brothers and sisters to African American males. It was not unusual for men to call the authors they were reading *my brother.* A professor from the University of Wisconsin writes how "every brother of the rooftop could quote Brother Fanon" (Van Deburg 1992). He was referring to Frantz Fanon, a

Caribbean-born author who wrote *The Wretched of the Earth* and *Black Skin, White Masks*. The quotation below from *Soul on Ice* is an example of accepting an author as a brother:

> Despite my rejection of [Thomas] Merton's theistic worldview, I could not keep him out of the room. He shouldered his way through the door. Welcome, Brother Merton. I give him a bear hug. (Cleaver 1968, 54)

Cleaver also describes how he liked Merton's description of a Harlem ghetto so much that he copied out the heart of it in longhand and kept the passage in mind whenever delivering Black Muslim lectures to other prisoners. Here is the passage:

> Here in this huge, dark, steaming slum, hundreds of thousands of Negroes are herded together like cattle, most of them with nothing to eat and nothing to do. All the senses and imagination and sensibilities and emotions and sorrows and desires and hopes and ideas of a race with vivid feelings and deep emotional reactions are forced in upon themselves, bound inward by an iron ring of frustration: the prejudice that hems them in with its four insurmountable walls. In this huge cauldron, inestimable natural gifts, wisdom, love, music, science, poetry are stamped down and left to boil with the dregs of an elementally corrupted nature, and thousands upon thousands of souls are destroyed by vice and misery and degradation, obliterated, wiped out, washed from the register of the living, dehumanized. (55)

After reading this passage in *Soul on Ice*, I purchased Merton's *The Seven Storey Mountain* (1948)—almost forty years later, Cleaver passed his brother author on to me. I was struck by other parts of Merton's text, particularly the excerpt below:

> For it had become evident to me that I was a great rebel. I fancied that I had suddenly risen above all the errors and stupidities and mistakes of modern society—there are enough of them to rise above, I admit—and that I had taken my place in the ranks of those who held up their heads and squared their shoulders and marched into the future. In the modern world, people are always holding up their heads and marching into the future, although they haven't the slightest idea what they think the "future" is or could possibly mean. The only future we seem to walk into,

in actual fact, is full of bigger and more terrible wars, wars well calculated
to knock our upraised heads off those squared shoulders. (103)

These words, which I discovered while writing this book, caused me think
about the warring of young souls who are moving toward the future with the
need to *raise their heads and square their shoulders* in order to become self-
determined.

Although Eldridge Cleaver initially tried to resist Merton's message ("I
could not keep him out of the room"), the text penetrated his thinking, left
him with fresh ideas, and impacted his life. Are we putting such penetrating
texts in front of, and discussing them with, African American adolescent
males? My examination of textual lineages over the past three years suggests
that we are not.

I wrote this poem to capture this need to help young African American
males find brother and sister authors they can collaborate around.

Brother Author
by Alfred W. Tatum

Are you out there?
Are you out there?
Putting your thoughts together for me
I want to situate myself comfortably in your pages
As you write about uncomfortable truths
You don't have to be nice to me
Just be fair
I can handle it

Are you out there?
Are you out there?
I woke up this morning expecting something good to happen
I knew I was going to find your words
Words that lift me up without tearing me down
I am waiting for you
Maybe you are already hidden in the stacks
Finish this for me www . . .
So that I can Google you

continues

Are you out there?
Are you out there?
Are you keeping up with what's happening to me?
Make sense of my actions so that I can act differently

Brother Author
Brother Author
Where are you?
My ears and heart are open
I know you know that I cry on my pillow at night
This is when my humanity comes to light—in my own personal darkness
I need to find you before my personal darkness becomes the world's darkness

I need to find you, Brother Author, so that I can find myself
I showed up again today and again nothing
I stared at the pages and I did not hear you speaking to me
You were not there to tell me who I am and what I can become

Tomorrow, Brother Author, I hope I find you
I am still looking, waiting, praying, crying
Until then, I just don't know.

Penetrating Texts

African American adolescent males today need the same thought-penetrating messages. Imagine these young men photocopying passages to place in their back pockets. Imagine educational publishers identifying or developing materials that prompt young men to rip out pages to keep with them. After reading *Forged by Fire* (Draper 1997), a student from a middle school in Boston, Massachusetts, wrote, "I need this book. I feel this book." This idea of providing texts that students need and want should guide the thinking of educators and educational publishers who want to reconnect adolescents with texts.

There is just-below-the-surface murmuring by educators and parents that African American adolescent males do not value reading. Admittedly, I have observed these young men reject reading over the past fifteen years. I have also watched them disconnect because of the way texts are mediated or discussed. However, I have *not* seen them devalue reading when the texts are interesting and provocative. This suggests that these young men do not devalue reading but devalue what they are required to read or how literary and nonliterary texts are mediated. This is an important distinction. Take the following series of emails, and the poetry written as a result, as an example.

Email, September 16, 2008

Hello, Dr Tatum,

. . . I am emailing you because I have a new job as the reading specialist in [X] school district and I teach reading class. . . . One of the required readings this fall is *Black Boy*, by Richard Wright, and my students are having a hard time getting into and digesting the text. I was wondering if you had any suggestions of activities I could do with them to help them navigate through the book and get the most out of it in some creative way. I have 22 students in my class and 14 of them are boys. HELP please.

Thanks in advance

◆ ◆ ◆ ◆ ◆

Response, September 16, 2008

Hi, Ms. [X],

To your question,
Black Boy is a long text that needs careful and critical mediation/discussion. The key is to consistently complement the text with other fast-moving pieces. A poem that captures the feelings of the characters in the book can be used. But more important, the text must be connected to questions that students find essential today.

For example, use the following passage as a text starter:

> Whenever I thought of the bleakness of black life in America, I knew that Negroes had never been allowed to catch the full spirit of Western Civilization, that they lived somehow in it but not of it. And when I brooded upon the cultural barrenness of black life, I wondered if clean, positive tenderness, love, honor, loyalty, and the capacity to remember were native to man. (37)

Then ask the following questions:

1. What's native to man? Meaning, what is born in us and what is not?
2. Is there such a thing as cultural barrenness? Of black life? Of white life? Of Asian life?

Activity: Have students capture Wright's feelings or the feelings of cultural barrenness in a poem. You may have to share your own writing with the students. This strengthens their engagement.

Lastly, I am attaching a framework I use for mediating/discussing text. I also frame my work around literacy platforms, that is, why am I asking the students to engage with the text? The framework is not specific to *Black Boy*. It's the structure that is most important.
Hope this helps.

Until next time,

Dr. Alfred W. Tatum

◆ ◆ ◆ ◆ ◆

Email, September 16, 2008

Dr. Tatum,

. . . Thanks for your help. The text was chosen for the students by a group of individuals that teach the reading classes. . . . It was intended to be an outside reading with no support. . . . I will use the information you gave me to help me structure this and future readings.
Again, thanks, Doc

God Bless

◆ ◆ ◆ ◆ ◆

Email, September 22, 2008

Dear Dr. Tatum,

I have attached a sample of the poetry my students generated around the first couple of chapters of *Black Boy*. It's amazing what students can do when given just a little push. They ranted and raved about not liking or understanding the text, but as you read their work, you can sense they pick up the theme. [Below are five poems from the reading specialist's eighth-period class]

Poem 1

Feeling lonely and cold, on my own
Having to take care of myself
Like I'm a man that's grown
Anger and wrath, built inside of me
I want to lock myself in a room
Or someone to hide me
No one to comfort me, no one to love me, I hate my dad
For what he did to me

◆ ◆ ◆

Poem 2

Lonely
Broke
Hungry
Scared
Cold
Angry
Sad
Invisible
No family by his side

Old
Poor
Homeless
Tired
Pain
Small in a big world

Poem 3

Lonely
Not there
Don't exist
In the shadow

Try to be "alive," but not on the right side
Try to be "there," but no existence
Look for a "light side," but still on the dark side
Try to be "heard," but still lonely

◆ ◆ ◆

Poem 4

Outraged
Discouraged
Infuriated
Trying to eat dinner without food on my plate
Angered
Provoked
Wrathful
Ignorance makes me feel like an animal
Indignant
Dispirited
Tormentness
Not having my father here gives me hopelessness

◆ ◆ ◆

Poem 5

Poverty
Hunger
Shame
Blame
Daddy's to blame
Living in fame
The pain
The rain
Is falling down . . .
I feel the name
Richard Wright.

Response, September 22, 2008

Hi, Ms. [X],

The writing of the young men is powerful. They have gifts that are often untapped, undiscovered. I am sitting here with my heart filled. Thanks for allowing the young men to put their voices on record. They need to continue to tell their stories and write their own lives. Continue to use texts in powerful ways and you will be instrumental in nurturing the next generation of nation builders. We must never let others convince us that our young men do not have promise, even the ones living in communities of turmoil. Continue to score with reading and writing and you will have a wonderful year. It's not just about their literacy development; it's about their lives!

Hail to the young men!

The notion that African American males do not value reading is pure speculation. It is difficult to value (or reject) something you have not fully experienced. Somehow, however, it is easy for educators to accept as fact that African American males living in poor communities devalue reading. Masking the pain or shame of not being able to read well is often misdiagnosed as devaluing reading. Having insufficient skills and strategies to comprehend texts embarrasses the hell out of adolescents. Skills and strategies are important, and there are plenty of books filled with them, but they are not enough. I am addressing the other part of the literacy development equation—the content of the texts boys are asked to read in school and how these texts are mediated and discussed. African American males may reject what they are asked to read because the material doesn't focus on their development in the context of their life and experiences.

The penetration of text that leads to new knowledge and fresh thinking occurs when students are taught, challenged, and valued. Unfortunately, as I describe later in this book, African American adolescent males are not reading academically, culturally, spiritually, and socially penetrating texts in school. This is due in large part, but not entirely, to a short-sighted focus on achieving minimum reading standards and test scores to satisfy school-based standards and requirements, a focus that can ultimately leave these young men underprepared for higher education. To be fair, severing texts from the lives of young black males preceded No Child Left Behind (NCLB) and the focus on minimum standards. And we educators, for a wide range of reasons, are complicit in this separation—inadvertent accomplices in depriving these young males of appropriate texts and curtailing their textual lineages.

Collaboration around texts—in formal and informal settings, inside and outside schools—has historically been part of the fiber of the literacy development of African American males. A middle-aged African American high school art teacher told me how he, as a high school student, rallied with other males to learn Rudyard Kipling's "If," a poem that is now part of his textual lineage.

This approach has been abandoned. Little, if any, collaboration takes place in schools around reading texts or writing pieces that pay attention to the context of the lives of African American adolescent males. This is an outgrowth of not having a clear definition of the role of literacy instruction for adolescents on a broader scale or a clear definition of the role of literacy instruction for African American adolescent males in particular. Therefore, these boys have no knowledge of their history of collaborating around texts, being part of a broader literacy community, or using and producing texts as a way to address issues related to their circumstances with the intent to find direction and dictate or define their future. They remain clueless to this past, which goes beyond a superficial, pride-building exercise and which was prevalent in both racially integrated and segregated schools of the past—a past littered with many racial constraints that do not exist today. Ultimately, they are left without a textual lineage.

An Institute Planned as a Literacy Collaborative

What might literacy as a collaborative act look like in practice? Based on the history of how African American males read and wrote texts, I designed a five-week African American Adolescent Male Summer Literacy Institute (AAAMSLI) for the University of Illinois at Chicago's Reading Clinic. Twelve African American young males, from various public schools in metropolitan Chicago, became part of a literacy collaborative aimed at becoming socially conscious readers and writers. They wrote poetry, short stories, children's stories, and the seeds of novels as part of this aim. During individual interviews, these young males of different ages and academic abilities unanimously mentioned that there was power in their working together. Each suggested that the length of the institute should be extended. They *all* called for more time to read and write together.

This is how I described the institute in a recruiting brochure:

The UIC Reading Clinic, under the direction of Dr. Alfred W. Tatum, will host its first African American Adolescent Male Summer Literacy Institute (AAAMSLI). AAAMSLI is for young men ages eleven through seventeen. The focus of the institute is reading and writing for social justice. Twelve African American adolescent males will be offered the opportunity to participate. With a special emphasis on urban youth, the institute will mentor future writers. A primary goal is nurturing the next generation of socially conscious readers and writers similar to the likes of James Baldwin, W. E. B. Du Bois, Ralph Ellison, Richard Wright, and the beloved young adult novelist, Walter Dean Myers.

The young men will read interesting and provocative texts and write with the aim of addressing critical issues affecting their generation. One potential source of publication for these aspiring writers is Scholastic's *Storyworks* magazines.

Interested young males were asked to complete the application shown in Figure 2.3 on page 35. I read all the writing samples submitted to gauge the issues the young males cared about. Two of the writing samples are included below. The first is by an applicant who chose option 2, the second by one who chose option 5.

Writing Sample 1

Bring on the Day!
Wake up wake up it's a new day
Preparing for the trials that come my way
Fiery darts I dodge so precisely aimed
Like drug abuse, hot girls, and gangs
It's easy to get distracted after being taught to paper chase
Trying to get some amazing grace
But it's hard to get favor 'cause of the complexion of my face
And on top of that most of us are the head of the house
Although we're too young to have a spouse
Forced quick to become a man

continues

But never taught to hold on to God's unchanging hand
Yet here I stand
With success and failure in each hand
Will I falter in my ways letting time go by like sand
But I tell myself NO! With the thunderous voice only a black man can
You see now I'm old enough to understand
That everything is possible with the right tools in your hand
So go head! Charge on! Because here I stand
Come forth try to do the worst you can
'Cause the war doesn't always go to the strongest man, but also to the one
    that can withstand
I'm ready! With more than just a fighting chance
Suited and booted in my fighting stance
You knocked me down once it's not gone be that easy again
And it's no secret you won't be victorious in the end
SO BRING ON THE DAY!!

Writing Sample 2

The three most pressing issues I see facing young men today are gang violence, underage sex, and drinking. In society, I see a lot of this. Really, out of all of these, I think gang violence is the most pressing issue.

To me, the reasons young men join gangs are because they feel they don't have any one at home they can relate or talk to, or they are seeking love, or there is no father present. Some other reasons could be all the violence young men watch on TV or their desire to be "cool."

Underage sex is another problem in society. Young men at my school are really worried about having sex and I don't understand why. I don't think sex is something to be worried about. I don't see what the rush is about. I think there is a time and place to do it, and right now is not the time for me or my peers to have sex. I also hear of guys buying condoms and others asking questions like "did you get in her panties yet?"—It's crazy! It's scary to think about what it would be like to be somebody's daddy at 14!

Drinking is a big issue as well. I feel that drinking can lead to gang violence and underage sex. Most young men get into drinking because of the influence of family and friends, especially friends. When you drink you are not thinking correctly. You are delirious and can make bad choices. You are insane.

African American Adolescent Male Summer Literacy Institute
at
University of Illinois at Chicago

Application

1. Applicant's Name _____ 2. Applicant's Age _____

3. Applicant's Home Address _____

   City _____ Zip Code _____

4. Applicant's School _____

5. Names of Parents/Guardians _____

6. Parent/Guardian Home Telephone _____ Cell Phone _____

   Emergency Contact Name: _____ Telephone _____

   E-mail contact: _____

For Applicant Only: Please select one of the options below to provide a writing sample.

Option 1: W. E. B. Du Bois wrote:

When a human being becomes suddenly conscious of the tremendous powers lying latent with him, when from the puzzled contemplation of a half-known self, he rises to the powerful assertion of self, conscious of his might, then there is loosed upon the world possibilities of good that make men pause.

What message was Du Bois trying to convey? Do you believe his message is relevant for African American males today? Why or why not?

Option 2: Write a poem (one page) or short story (three to five pages) that captures a contemporary African American male experience.

Option 3: Describe the most interesting and provocative book, poem, or essay you have read to date, and explain why the text was interesting and provocative.

Option 4: In 200–400 words, describe what you believe it means to be socially conscious.

Option 5: Identify the three most pressing issues you see facing young men in today's society.

Option 6: Writers have used several descriptors in relation to African American males. Among them is the word *monster*. In your own words, unpack the validity of this descriptor.

Option 7: Submit a writing sample of your choice.

Fig. 2.3: *AAAMSLI Application*

When I think about these three pressing issues, I see that the common bond between them is peer pressure. Peer pressure is the cause of gang violence, underage sex, and drinking in young men. So, although I named three pressing issues, peer pressure is at the base of them all.

Each of the selected participants received the following letter:

Dear [Student Name],

Congratulations! You have been selected to participate in this year's African American Adolescent Male Summer Literacy Institute (AAAMSLI) at the University of Illinois at Chicago (UIC). You will have the opportunity to work with other young men who expressed an interest to read and write for social justice. I cannot express enough how excited I am for the opportunity to introduce you to a wide range of texts and help you begin to put your voice on record.

The AAAMSLI at UIC will begin on July 1 and end on July 31. We will meet at the UIC Reading Clinic from 1 p.m. to 4 p.m. on Tuesday, Wednesday, and Thursday during the first four weeks. We will interact online during the last week as you complete your culminating writing project.

During the institute, you will develop and extend your writing by studying and critiquing the works of authors such as James Baldwin, Amiri Baraka, Countee Cullen, Ralph Ellison, Langston Hughes, James Weldon Johnson, Claude McKay, Walter Dean Myers, Richard Wright, and many others. These authors, past and present, will serve as our language coaches and writing mentors as we write about contemporary issues affecting African American adolescent males. It is my hope that this year's inaugural institute will be an intense but fun and provocative experience for you.

As a member of the institute, you will be given a stipend of $150. That's right, you will be paid to write. Additionally, you will have exclusive rights to the AAAMSLI blog, where you will interact with the institute leader and other institute members.

You and your parents are invited to attend a one-hour orientation on June 25, 2008, at 3 p.m., at the UIC Reading Clinic to receive more information about the African American Adolescent Male Summer Literacy Institute. You will receive an outline of the institute at the orientation. The UIC Reading Clinic is located at 1040 W. Harrison in the EPASW Building (corner of Harrison and Morgan), Room L268. The telephone number is (312) 996-0709.

Again, congratulations. I look forward to meeting you on June 25, 2008.

Dr. Alfred W. Tatum
Director of the UIC Reading Clinic

The following outline was provided during the orientation:

Five Writing Frames Around Issues of Social Justice

⇒ Poetic Broadsides—Week 1
⇒ Black Shorts—Week 2
⇒ Children's Book—Week 3
⇒ Essay—Week 4
⇒ First Chapter of a Novel—Week 5

Four Platforms for Progress

⇒ Defining self
⇒ Becoming resilient
⇒ Engaging others
⇒ Building capacity

The young men received thirteen texts to read during the institute, selected to align with students' voices as reflected in the writing samples submitted with their applications. These texts were also the mentor texts for the five writing frames and the four platforms for progress mentioned above.

1. *Wings*, by Christopher Myers

2. *Black Boy*, by Richard Wright

3. *The Best Negro Short Stories*, by Langston Hughes

4. *The First Part Last*, by Angela Johnson

5. *Pass It On: African American Poetry for Children*, by Wade Hudson

6. *Be Boy Buzz*, by bell hooks

7. *Locomotion*, by Jacqueline Woodson

8. *Vintage Hughes*, a collection of the work of Langston Hughes

9. *The Classic Slave Narratives*, edited by Henry Louis Gates

10. *Sounder*, by William Armstrong

11. *The Fire Next Time*, by James Baldwin

12. *Bronzeville Boys and Girls*, by Gwendolyn Brooks

13. *A Raisin in the Sun*, by Lorraine Hansberry

The young males also received templates they could use to help structure their writing. I told them often, "You can't write about you if you don't know about you." On the third day of the institute, for example, they were given a template to prompt initial research that would help them plan their writing (see Figure 2.4).

They also used templates that prompted them to read as writers. For example, I would ask them to explain what they believed the authors needed to know in order to write their text. They responded to this question after examining this poem, one of the first they read.

Untitled (1967)
by Don L. Lee (now Haki Madhubuti)

America calling.
negroes.
can you dance?
play foot/baseball?
nanny?
cook?
needed now. negroes
who can entertain
ONLY.
others not wanted.
(& are considered extremely dangerous.)

FACTS ABOUT AFRICAN AMERICAN ADOLESCENT MALES	MYTHS ABOUT AFRICAN AMERICAN ADOLESCENT MALES	AFRICAN AMERICAN ADOLESCENT MALES AND EDUCATION	*CHATHAM NORTH LAWNDALE BRONZEVILLE WEST PULLMAN GARFIELD PARK

* Chicago communities in which the students resided

Fig. 2.4: *AAAMSLI Planning-to-Write Matrix*

The students also received "brother author" rubrics (see Figure 2.5 on page 40), which they used to critique all the writing they did in response to the assigned texts, as well as the writings of the other brother authors participating in the institute.

Productive Starting Points

Reconceptualizing literacy as a collaborative act with and among African American adolescent males and helping them identify brother and sister authors are productive starting points for addressing their literacy needs. Five practical steps are involved in shaping literacy collaboratives:

Brother Author _____ Date _____

SELF-REGULATION/EVALUATION	PEER RATING
Organization: The events follow a logical sequence.	4 3 2 1 0
Interest Level/Momentum: The story is interesting and keeps the reader involved.	4 3 2 1 0
Situated: The story is clearly situated in a time and place.	4 3 2 1 0
Authenticity: The story seems real and believable.	4 3 2 1 0
Care: The author took care to provide the necessary details.	4 3 2 1 0
Word Choice: The author chose words that capture the reader, and words that seem to fit.	4 3 2 1 0
Voice: The voice seems real and authentic.	4 3 2 1 0
Total	

Additional Comments to the Brother Author

Fig. 2.5: *Brother Author Rubric*

1. *Anchor reading and writing instruction in clearly defined platforms* that will allow them to benefit in racially segregated and racially integrated settings.
   a. defining self
   b. becoming resilient
   c. engaging others
   d. building capacity for change

   Use the platforms as critical-thought points for identifying, selecting, and mediating texts in ways that pay attention to fair and equitable treatment, coexistence, and being progressive in society.

2. *Identify essential questions* that capture their attention.
   a. How does racial and social isolation affect one's identity?
   b. Should everyone, including illegal immigrants and those convicted of felonies, be able to participate in America's democracy?
   c. Many descriptors have been used to describe African American males. Among the descriptors is *invisible man*. Is this a valid descriptor?
   d. Do we control or negotiate our destiny?

   The second question would trigger a better conversation about democracy than asking students "What is a democracy?" because it contextualizes democracy and could lead them to examine why, in some states, one out of four African American males are denied their right to vote (Manza and Uggen 2006). What factors cause voters to make decisions along racial lines? Tap into the pressing issues African American adolescent males face in school and society as a way to construct essential questions.

3. *Identify texts that engage.* Identify texts—literary and nonliterary, conventional and nonconventional—that are fast moving, deeply penetrating, and relevant to the essential questions. Lead students in discussing the texts, making sure to honor their voices while finding your own voice as an educator of young people around complex issues. The texts can include protest poetry of the Harlem Renaissance and the 1960s (Reid 2002). (Chapter 6 is an extended discussion about poetry.)

4. *Move beyond texts that only stress a victim mentality* to include texts that focus on self-reliance, resilience, and self-determination. Texts cannot

focus solely on young black males who need societal intervention to counteract their lack of an individual work ethic and sense of personal responsibility.

5. *Structure platforms of action.* Encourage students to do something with the new information they are learning. For example, have the young males create literacy clubs or action plans that will improve their literacy as they use it to support real action and dialogue; don't let literacy become just a symbolic victory.

There is ample historical precedent for shaping literacy as a collaborative act among African American males. History suggests it is imperative to identify meaningful texts that pay attention to their lives inside and outside school. We must begin to wrestle with this question: Out of all of the texts in the world, why do we want to put these texts in front of African American adolescent males living in economically deprived communities? More simply, if I had to choose only four or five texts to use with my students, which texts would I use? To answer these questions, we must listen to their voices and pay attention to their experiences as they navigate communities of turmoil. However, structuring literacy as a collaborative act will not be enough to address the reading needs of young males who live complex lives. There are other vital signs of literacy development to consider.

Vital Signs of Literacy Development

> Sometimes I feel like a motherless child a long way from home.
>
> —JAMES WELDON JOHNSON

> When he was younger, Carl would hide letters announcing events at school, because he didn't want anyone asking him why his mother wasn't there. "I like being quiet and writing raps," he said. "I don't like to talk much, 'cause all the kids that I'm around—they live the natural life [with their parents], by me growing up so different, we don't have much to talk about."
>
> —NELL BERNSTEIN

Literacy reform efforts that do not pay attention to reading and writing, the reader and the writer, reading and writing instruction, and educators' approaches to literacy development will fail. Current approaches to educating African American adolescent males from high-poverty communities who struggle with reading and writing are incorrect. The gap in reading achievement between African American males and other students after fourth grade is not natural. There is a problem with the usual paths set out for African American males in the system. They are:

1. Placed in middle and high school remedial reading programs

2. Required to attend tutoring or other in-school support sessions

3. Given simpler texts

These solutions are not working because they are shortsighted and focus on helping students become better readers without clearly defining the role of literacy in their lives. Even though the reading achievement gap persists, educators and policy makers continue to try to make these failed approaches work by providing professional development or reorganizing schools (America's newest educational rallying cries), instead of seeking different, more comprehensive solutions to advance the literacy development of these young males. Solutions have to focus on the vital signs of literacy development (Tatum 2008).

1. *Vital signs of reading and writing*—the working tools (decoding, self-questioning, using language, monitoring comprehension, summarizing, other strategies) students need to handle and produce text independently—are the necessary minimum. Sadly, this is where many current literacy reform efforts begin and end.

2. *Vital signs of readers and writers* are related to students' lived experiences both inside and outside school; they reflect an improved human condition.

3. *Vital signs of reading and writing instruction* are intimately related to rescuing and refining the *significance* of literacy instruction and helping us conceptualize the rationale for providing it. Educators must focus on appropriate texts, quality support, assessments, and the potential uses of technology in order to maximize opportunities to shape rigorous adolescent literacy.

4. *Vital signs of educators' approaches.* Educational contexts must be characterized by caring, commitment, competence, and culpability. Adolescents benefit when they know they belong in the learning environment, experience psychosocial membership in the learning community, and feel they are in the presence of an adult advocate who is not going to give up on them (Goodenow 1993; Price 2000).

These vital signs call attention to four corresponding gaps—a reading achievement gap, a relationship gap, a rigor gap, and a responsiveness gap—that affect students' literacy (see Figure 3.1).

READING AND WRITING	READERS AND WRITERS	READING AND WRITING INSTRUCTION	EDUCATORS' APPROACHES
Providing the tools/models	Improving the human condition	Rescuing the significance of teaching	Interacting with students, not scorecards of achievement
(What)	(Why)	(How)	(Who)
Word knowledge Fluency Strategy knowledge Writing Language	Home life Culture Environment Language Economics	Quality instructional support Text Context Assessment Technology	Competence Commitment Caring Culpability
Reading Gap	**Relationship Gap**	**Rigor Gap**	**Response Gap**

Fig. 3.1: *Vital Signs of Literacy Development*

The vital signs of literacy development are essential for equipping African American adolescents with skills and strategies and engaging them with texts in the classroom (Tatum 2008). Disdain for the curriculum leads African American adolescent males to disengage in the classroom (Price 2000); eventually many of these young males drop out of high school (Murtadha-Watts 2000). African American adolescent males who struggle with reading need the combination of *powerful instruction* (skills and strategies) and *powerful texts* to enable and engage them in developmentally appropriate ways.

Literacy instruction for African American adolescent males has to have the ring of truth. W. E. B. Du Bois (2001) best described the role of literacy instruction for African American males when he stated:

On one point, therefore, there can be no question—no hesitation: unless we develop [their] full capabilities, [they] cannot survive. If [they] are to be trained grudgingly and suspiciously; trained not with reference to what [they] can be, but with sole reference to what somebody wants [them] to be; if instead of following the methods pointed out by the accumulated wisdom of the world for the development of full human power, we simply are trying to follow the line of least resistance and teach black men only such things and by such methods as are momentarily popular, then my fellow teachers, we are going to fail ignominiously in our attempt to raise the black race to its full humanity and with that failure falls the fairest and fullest dream of a great united humanity. (26)

Parental Involvement or Lack Thereof

The tragic reality for many African American adolescent males is that they have to move toward a future in which others, perhaps even their parents, are already sure they will fail. I am often asked how I persuaded their parents to support the literacy development of the young males I taught. I did so by providing instruction that changed their sons. Parents wanted to find out about the teacher who was getting their sons to read books at home and use rich language. I used my students as conduits to get to know their parents.

I maintain that educators cannot allow a lack of parental support to rob these young males of their right to become highly literate. Literacy has to be thrust upon them—in some cases despite the lack of support they receive at home. Some parents of African American adolescent males who struggle with reading expect teachers to take responsibility for their sons' lives because of their own sense of defeat, as touched on in this email from a middle school teacher:

Hello, Dr. Tatum,

. . . This has been one of the most challenging years that I have experienced while teaching at the middle school level. I am seeing more minority children at lower reading levels and no home support. This concerns me deeply. I continue to make reading a priority every day by giving "my children" opportunities to experience what I call "successful literacy." I do have a group of males (12–13 years old) who are not motivated to do much of anything. Right now we are reading *We Beat the Street* and *Handbook for Boys* in small groups. I hope this experience allows them to see a light to make connections in their own lives. I must say that

I am disappointed in the lack of parent involvement or concern that these children have. When I call home to contact parents about positive days and struggling days, I get comments such as, "It's just a matter of time before he fails again," or "At this point I give up, he's your problem." As I spend nights rethinking new strategies and engaging lifelong lessons that deal with content, I take on each day as a new opportunity. I go into my class with the hope that this might be the one day I make a difference for one child. I refer back to your book often for encouragement and strength; most of all, it reminds me that I am not in this struggle alone. I just wanted to touch base with you to wish you and your family happy, healthy, and peaceful holidays. I hope one day we can meet to discuss these and other issues in more depth. Until then, my dream of "teaching black males to read" continues. . . .

In other situations, parents simply do not have stable enough lives themselves to support their sons or daughters. As an eighth-grade teacher, I was responsible for teaching a young male whose mother was a prostitute walking the streets a short distance from the school. One evening, four of his classmates had sex with his mother. I discovered in a phone call from him nine years later that this young man viewed my instruction and the reading materials I provided as sustaining forces that allowed him to persevere in the face of these degrading circumstances. He had Googled my name because he wanted to let me know that he was an engineering major at a highly respected university. He spoke of the poem "Test of a Man" and how he held on to it to get him through. I was close to tears by the time we hung up. I could only think of the advice my former elementary school principal gave me when I started teaching in an economically deprived community: "Let no one or nothing make you a poor teacher." I took this to mean poverty, poor parenting, and students (who because of a host of factors that weigh on the human soul) have a poor concept of who they are and what they can become.

Oversimplification and Underestimation

Although the above example is extreme, there are a host of factors that affect students' lives that should give educators pause when a skill-and-strategy focus is offered as the sole remedy. Nell Bernstein (2005) helps us understand one painful reality true for many of America's children in her book *All Alone in the World*. Almost two and a half million American children have a mother or father in jail. "As many as half of all adolescents whose parents do time will wind up behind bars themselves—a formula that virtually guarantees one generation's prison boom will feed and fuel the next" (3). The refueling is most prevalent among African American males.

Incarceration is only one devastating pattern found in high-poverty communities. Many other environmental factors (positive and negative) related to home life, culture, language, and economics impact the literacy development of African American adolescent males. Although all these young males do not respond to aversive events in the same way, their literacy development is intimately connected to everything that happens in their world.

Educators' efforts to address the literacy needs of African American adolescent males suffer from *underestimation* and *oversimplification* in four major areas.

1. *The efforts are rooted in the idea that all children are the same.* All children are not the same, and they do not receive the same treatment in school. Following a lesson I taught using excerpts from *A Raisin in the Sun* (Hansberry 1959), *Kaffir Boy* (Mathabane 1986), and *Shame of a Nation* (Kozol 2005), a group of high school students of diverse ethnic backgrounds told me that their "existence" in school is different—that they are treated differently because of race, class, and ability; that apartheid schooling exists in their building. Still, many educators ignore structural racism and refuse to see how schools create barriers for African American males. I am not arguing that African American adolescent males should be absolved of their responsibility in school, only that educators must acknowledge that school structures constructed by policy makers impact students' literacy development, both positively and negatively.

2. *The efforts are rooted in undergraduate and graduate teacher education programs that do not sufficiently prepare teachers to understand the multidisciplinary nature of literacy instruction.* While colleges of education are increasingly focused on preparing teachers to provide a high-quality education to an increasingly diverse student population, they are failing to prepare them to teach African American male adolescents from high-poverty communities. In higher education, conversations about

teaching reading to African American adolescent males are fractured, if not altogether absent. This is true in part because there is limited research on the literacy of African American adolescent males. I never had one conversation about teaching reading and writing to African American young males in reading methods courses in my undergraduate or graduate programs. I only recall discussing these young males as "at risk" in educational psychology courses. Preservice teachers are not talking across disciplines (sociology, history, economics, philosophy, etc.) in many reading methods courses. As a result, the focus on improving reading achievement has been limited to using research-based skills and strategies and incorporating multicultural literature.

3. *We do not have the language necessary to discuss the literacy development of African American adolescent males.* The language we have too often ignores the broader context of their lives. It functions solely as a socially and politically expedient rallying cry. The field of literacy has been trapped behind reductive catchphrases such as *no child left behind, close the racial reading achievement gap*, and *every teacher is a reading teacher*. Despite our attempts to use language to shape practice, we have been unable to effectively teach reading to African American adolescent males who enter middle schools and high schools as struggling readers. Pessimism related to teaching these young males continues to grow. We need to expand both our conversations about the literacy development of African American adolescent males and the language we use in those conversations. The current superficial analysis often leads us to misinterpret the reading-related difficulties of African American adolescent males in middle school and high school classrooms. If we are serious about educating all of our nation's children we have to fashion smarter solutions across all disciplines.

4. *The efforts lack commitment.* Teaching African American adolescent males living in economically deprived communities requires commitment in the face of opposition. Many educators simply do not see the need to give concentrated attention to improving the reading achievement of these young males. Following a keynote presentation I delivered at the State Reading Association Conference in New York in 2006, a vendor told me that

> people refuse to buy your book [*Teaching Reading to Black Adolescent Males*] because they see black adolescents in the title. They

believe that there is no difference teaching black males and other students. You might want to think about not including black males [in the title] if you write another book.

I also received an email from a teacher in January 2007 that reflects the sentiments held by some educators *who are tired of talking about African American males.* The teacher wrote:

Dr. Tatum,

At our faculty meeting yesterday, my principal handed out copies of your book *Teaching Reading to Black Adolescent Males* for us to read. I inwardly groaned and took a copy.

Ironically, the teacher added, "I teach at an inner-city middle school in Huntsville, Alabama. Ninety-eight percent of the students receive free lunch and the student population is a combination of African American, Hispanic, Thai, American Indian, and white." She teaches in a community of turmoil where African American males are present and was *still* reluctant to read the text. Three weeks later, I received a second email from this same teacher asking me to provide professional development sessions at the school because the African American adolescent males did not meet adequate yearly progress. But I was asked not to mention African American males in the title of the presentation—just adolescent males. Other teachers from other school districts have expressed similar feelings.

- ◆ "Why are you talking about African American adolescent males?"
- ◆ "You are really talking about a class issue, not a race issue."
- ◆ "I did not think I was going to find anything valuable for my classroom, because of your focus on African American adolescent males."

In this nation, there is still a need to provide reasons for specifically addressing the needs of African American adolescent males when the data are clear—many of these young males are underperforming on reading and writing assessment and remain disconnected from reading and writing as part of their development. This is akin to asking a medical professional to explain her focus on breast cancer research because there are other types of deadly cancers.

Squeezing Teaching and Texts

Educators must courageously accept that we are part of a social and educational system that contributes to the underperformance of African American adolescent males. These young males are not failing on their own simply because they love failure or want to spite others. If African American adolescent males, as a group, have the track record of failure in school that they do, it is reasonable to conclude that educators are part of the system failing them. African American males are not engaged in a great conspiracy to fail themselves. They do not enter kindergarten with the intent of becoming failures. My five-year-old son, getting off the bus after a day in kindergarten, blurted out, "I love school, Dad." This is a commonplace sentiment expressed by children starting kindergarten, *even African American boys.*

The failure of African American adolescent males is not their failure alone, but the failure of educators and parents to help them view academic success as a possibility. This is why we are ethically and morally obligated to speak the truth about gender, race, social class, and literacy development in the United States. One of the first steps is paying attention to the vital signs of literacy instruction discussed in this chapter.

Although I didn't fully realize it at the time, the vital signs of literacy development informed my practice as a teacher of adolescents. As an eighth-grade teacher, I resented the fact that my African American boys made me an "at-risk teacher." I was "at risk" of failing them if my teaching didn't enable them to absorb the curriculum. To solve my "at riskness," I had to care about my students despite their underperformance on reading-related tasks, the tough exterior they projected, their adolescent immaturity, the resistance they displayed, and the challenges they posed to my teaching. Most important, I had to study and work hard to provide responsive instruction.

I recall being challenged by a fifteen-year-old who asked, "Why do you get so upset when we don't do the work? You act like we're trying to hurt somebody." I do not recall how I responded, but I know I did not let the young male off the hook. I believed he was hurting himself, and that prompted me to squeeze my teaching and the texts in the curriculum for every ounce of possibility they contained. It is my hope that through this book, other teachers will find a way to squeeze texts for every ounce of possibility they contain to advance the literacy development of African American adolescent males.

Productive Starting Points

We need to achieve a balance between *strategies that enable* and *texts that engage.* I propose four solutions for enabling and engaging students.

1. *Develop expert procedures for teaching reading and writing and selecting useful texts.* Reading and writing cannot be taught with good intentions alone; knowledge and training are required.

2. *Systematize reading instruction.* Teachers of struggling readers need to establish a consistent instructional and assessment routine. Adolescents should know what to expect during reading and writing instruction and how they will be assessed afterward. Teachers need to say, "Today I am going to show you how to do thus-and-so"—to provide clear expectations for each lesson and remove the mystery that leaves many struggling readers confused. Struggling readers and writers need routine, repetitive instruction that is not boring.

3. *Focus on academic excellence and identity development.* The texts selected for adolescents need to pay attention to their multiple identities.

4. *Question disharmony.* Whenever reading and writing problems persist for groups of students, something is being undertreated or overlooked. We need to examine educational policies, teachers' behavior and disposition, instructional decisions, curriculum, plans of action, how literacy instruction is conceptualized and practiced, and how to ensure the necessary human and financial resources for success.

PART II:
ENABLING TEXTS

Characteristics and Examples of Enabling Texts

■ **Essential question for students and educators:** How does a person become reconciled to a strange land?

What makes an educated citizen?

> We hold these truths to be self-evident that all Men are created equal …
>
> —THE DECLARATION OF INDEPENDENCE

> You had far better all die—die immediately, he told them, than to live to be slaves.
>
> —HENRY HIGHLAND GARNETT

We need to (re)connect African American adolescent males with texts in order to begin shaping a positive life trajectory for them. Unless powerful texts anchor literacy reform—texts that are models of rich language—these young men will continue to be underserved in schools. They must be enabled and engaged by texts mediated by educators who use these texts to broker positive relationships and improve their lives.

An Historical Look at Enabling Texts

Arguably, one of the most important texts for African American males during the late eighteenth and early nineteenth centuries were these thirty-six words found in the Declaration of Independence:

We hold these truths to be self-evident that all Men are created equal, that they are endowed by their Creator with certain unalienable Rights, that among these are Life, Liberty, and the Pursuit of Happiness.

With the exception of the Old Testament and maybe the *Original Blue Back Speller* (Webster 1824/2002), the Declaration of Independence moved African American males toward action like no other written text. This document gave them a foothold from which to challenge the hypocrisy of America's founding fathers. It moved them to act more forcibly on their own behalf with a boldness and an unabated ferocity using the language of the Declaration of Independence with passion and great intensity.

For example, the abolitionist David Walker, in his *Appeal to the Coloured Citizens of the World*, "took the Declaration's rhetoric of equality and—as many black abolitionists would continue to do—turned it to his own end, effectively chastising a nation of hypocrites and openly challenging the racist status quo" (Johnson and Smith 1998, 342). Walker believed in the unalienable rights cited in the Declaration of Independence, as evidenced by these words:

> [It is] an unshaken and forever immovable fact, that your full glory and happiness, as well as all other coloured people under Heaven, shall never be fully consummated, [without] the entire emancipation of your enslaved brethren all over the world. (343)

It is believed that David Walker was poisoned for writing a text aimed at encouraging and demanding that blacks, both free and enslaved, strike down injustices that trapped them in a system of oppression and degradation. When warned by friends to leave for Canada to avoid death at the hands of white men from Georgia, Walker stated:

> I will stand my ground. Somebody must die in this cause. I may be doomed to the stake and the fire, or to scaffold tree, but it is not in me to falter if I can promote the work of emancipation. (343)

The Declaration of Independence and Walker's *Appeal* are *enabling texts* that led African American males to act on their own lives. Walker's writings insisted and demanded that blacks

1. take a critical look at their oppression and oppressors,

2. exercise solidarity,

3. value education, and

4. treasure their link to an African homeland.

His advocacy for these aims was directly related to the societal contexts of the late 1820s. His writings provided a *road map* and a *plan of action*. As the United States was contemplating removing blacks from the United States and exporting them to Sierra Leone, he wrote:

> Let no man of us budge one step. . . . America is more our country than it is the whites'. . . . The greatest riches in all America have arisen from our blood and tears: and will they drive us from our property and homes? . . . They must look sharp or this very thing will bring swift destruction upon them. Americans have got so fat on our blood and groans, that they have almost forgotten the God of armies. . . . They want us for their slaves, and think nothing of murdering us . . . therefore, if there is an attempt made by us, kill or be killed . . . and believe this, that it is no more harm for you to kill a man who is trying to kill you, than it is for you to take a drink of water when thirsty. (Johnson and Smith 1998, 341)

Parallel Texts for Today

History is laden with these types of *enabling texts* for African American males. However, there are no modern-day parallels being used in U.S. schools for African American adolescent males who need texts with similar *enabling* characteristics and who need *the language* to help them respond to their modern-day societal contexts, which may include living in economically deprived communities and receiving a second-rate education. They also need the language (and models of ways in which it can be used) to express their viewpoints and define who they are, as informed by their many and varied contexts. We need to ask young African American adolescent males the following questions:

1. What is the political, economic, and cultural significance of language?

2. How does a global *majority* become a national *minority*?

We need to ask ourselves:

1. What knowledge or language do they need to respond to these questions in intelligent ways in both writing and speech?

2. What texts will allow them to do so and will be *useful* to them as they try to navigate the questions that shape their existence?

Using David Walker's enabling text as a prototype, I wrote this example of an enabling text that can be used today.

An Appeal to African American Male Students Who Struggle in School
by Alfred W. Tatum

You must avoid becoming a victim of a meaningless existence. It is your responsibility to fight against ignorance and shallow thinking and strike against poor academic performance. Question what you are being offered in school. For example, ask your teachers, "How will this education you are offering me contribute to my survival and the survival of future generations?" Ask, "How will this education move me toward a position of influence in my local, national, and global community?" Tell them to be specific; do not accept fluff. Ask the same of your administrators as you rally outside their doors. If you do not do this and demand real answers, you allow others to fail you as you add to your own failure. It is your responsibility to seek knowledge to achieve your God-given rights. No more self-pity. No more silence. Speak up and demand excellence from others and yourself. If you fail to do this, you are the fool who robs himself of the right to full citizenship and participation in the society in which you were born and live. This makes you a criminal of humanity and deserving of everything that happens to you. The time for being slow-walked through school and life has passed. You were not born to receive a second-rate education. You were not born to do as little as possible to get by. You must become dissatisfied with these things right away. You do not have a moment to waste. Rally together with others who are interested in changing your condition, black, white, brown, it doesn't matter. Someone among you must share this message with others until they understand you. Do not be afraid. You deserve better and God expects that you take your rightful place in life. I pray that you understand this message and start working to fulfill your destiny now. If not, you are doomed and have no one to blame but yourself. You must collaborate to ensure your victory. Do not be afraid. Start right now.

A ninth-grade reading teacher allowed me to use this text with his students. Within five minutes of reading the text, a white male student in the class raised his hand and challenged the teacher: how will this education you are offering me contribute to my survival and the survival of future generations? The teacher laughed, but I did not see it as a laughing matter; the young man deserved an answer, or he should have been directed to sources he could use to seek the answer.

Fear of and Resistance to Using Enabling Texts

Educators might find the text above to be incendiary and refuse to use it in largely segregated or largely integrated schools because of its expressed focus on African American adolescent males. Its usefulness in improving a reading score or satisfying a standard—two galvanizing forces in educating African American adolescent males who struggle with reading—may also be questioned. Teachers in schools where a large percentage of the African American adolescent males are underperforming may refuse to use texts with clear, pointed language—like the passage below:

> Some of you say, "But you don't know how colored people treat me sometimes. You know, man, black folks give me a harder time than white folks do. I try to help them and they fight me." But all of us are suffering from the same disease. It's called "plantation psychosis" and we have a serious mental disorder. We are working toward our destruction without realizing it. It is important to understand that when African people are in opposition to themselves they are mentally ill. That's what mental illness is. When you work against your own survival, you are crazy. (Akbar 1991, 31)

If this is the case, we have to seriously question and critique the role of literacy instruction and how it is being conceptualized in the United States for these young males.

Administrators may oppose using certain texts with African American adolescent males even when the young males find the text engaging. Here's an email I received from a teacher:

Dr. Tatum,

I had the privilege of hearing you speak at the IRA (International Reading Association) convention this past May. I can appreciate what you touch on; I myself am a middle school teacher with a goal to promote literacy. My students live in [a large urban city] on one of the roughest sides of town and come to school already programmed for failure. For the past year I have been looking for ways to get my students motivated to read and write. They write some amazing things, but when I push them to read, I am met with a great deal of resistance. I have taken into account what was said at the conference; that students read things they relate to. So with that in mind I have started to compile a list of books that have an urban flare to them. My principal is already questioning my tactic. One book in particular is a [author's name] novel. [The principal] does not believe the subject matter is appropriate. . . . I left the books out in my classroom and my students picked them up and started to read this particular book all on their own. When I collected the book because I had not finished reading it myself, a group of students went out and bought it themselves. Before long one student after another was reading the book and passing it off to their friends [pass-along reading, which I mentioned in a previous chapter]. My principal did not like this and believes I promoted the book to the students. I explained the situation to [the principal] and [the principal] has suggested that [we] go over my booklist this summer. . . . How do I prepare myself to defend my booklist, because I fear that [the principal] does not understand that the students' reality is different from what [we] would like to dream it is and that my students are exposed to many things that we as educators would like to believe they are not? I understand as an educator that getting students to pass standardized tests is important, but at the same time, the fact that the students picked up this book without encouragement from me and were self-driven tells me that some books need to be on my booklist even though they may be a little racy.

The refusal to use texts focused on strengthening the minds of African American adolescent males in today's schools is no less damaging than the prohibition of incendiary texts during one of the darkest points in U.S. history when laws were in place to prohibit any black person from learning to read. It was believed that reading would impair their value as slaves and destroy their contentedness. Today's educators have accepted the idea that the African

American adolescent male reading problem is here to stay. This perpetuates the status quo. Educators, en masse, have not become bold or astute enough to use texts to shatter the contentedness they observe among the young males. The literacy development of African American males in the United States suffers as a result.

A False Dichotomy

The primary barrier to selecting and using texts aimed at strengthening the minds of African American adolescent males, particularly in integrated schools, is the resistance by school boards, administrators, teachers, and parents who do not (or do not want to) understand why certain texts have to be selected expressly for African American males. This fear or refusal needs to be challenged. During a professional development inservice I conducted at a high school, I was told that if the teachers began using texts that focused on building consciousness among African American male students, white parents would pull their white children out. The comment was made publicly, and no one attempted to rebut it, so I asked, "So what do we do, continue to fail *certain* students because we fear how *certain* parents will react?"

This false dichotomy, based on a superficial analysis, is often invoked—but switching the focus to the literacy needs of *all* students prevents or obscures the literacy development of *certain* students. The literacy development of the collective cannot be addressed without addressing the literacy development of the individual. The theoretically humanistic claim that we must focus on *all* is less humanistic in practice if the literacy needs of *certain* students are not fully addressed. As a result, schools are not using texts conceptualized to build consciousness that will lead to self-determination among African American adolescent males as they move toward manhood.

I am not advocating texts that insert a wedge in interracial relationships. However, it is important to have African American males read texts that respond to their needs. Below is a chapter from my unpublished novel *Chip Chop*:

Race(ism)
by Alfred W. Tatum

You discover more about yourself in unfamiliar territories than in familiar ones. Stepping outside yourself requires real risks. But people stop entering races because they have become accustomed to losing. They do not want to race anymore. Instead, they say that the race does not matter when they are in last place. That's a stupid race, they say.

I get like this sometimes. If I do not win something, I notice I say "forget it" the next time. Like in third grade, I lost the multiplication bee. I did not enter the next year. But I was mouthing all of the answers at my desk while the other students were standing in the front of the room. I remember telling Lance, "I would've won if I was in it." All he asked was, "Why didn't you get in?" I told him that the math bee was stupid when I really didn't feel that way. Although I know I am the best writer in the classroom, I also didn't enter the essay contest last month because I lost to Alex earlier this year. Mr. Tillman tried to encourage me. I just told him that I wasn't feeling the essay contest's theme—The Good and Bad of Technology in Urban Communities. Mr. Tillman's college roommate asked our class to enter the contest. He worked for a major technology company that was trying to get kids in the city to use computers more. He visited our classroom and talked about the technology gap and how our school only had sixteen computers for 542 students. But I didn't enter the contest out of fear of losing to Alex again. I took myself out of the race. This gave me no chance of winning. Never again. Mr. Tillman is saying time is up. So I am up. Check you later, journal. Until next time, peace.

Today, we talked about race(ism) in class. This is not like racism that exists between groups, but race(ism) that has to do with individuals. This surprised us because we were used to talking about racism between groups in the United States in our social studies class. Racism between black and whites. Racism between Germans and Jews.

We entered the classroom and saw the word *also-ran* on the board. Mr. Tillman started talking about horses and stuff. He explained that winning horses need also-rans to build their confidence. You see, also-rans never win races. No matter how much they compete, they keep losing. Then, people come to expect these horses to keep losing. Stallions look down on them. Thoroughbreds appear to be more graceful. Also-rans exist to be losers.

While Mr. Tillman was talking, Hank looked the word up in the dictionary. He always does this to see if what a teacher is saying is true. Mr. Tillman told us to *be* walking dictionaries, but Hank believed it was better to walk *with* a dictionary just in case his memory failed him. At the end of the year he will probably win the prize for the most used, crumbly, torn, ripped-pages, thumbed-through, trying-to-prove-somebody-wrong dictionary user. Hank read the definition: "also-ran, noun, 1. a horse that does not win, place, or show in a race 2. a loser in a competition 3. one that has little talent or success." Hank had his own way of reading definitions. He stated the part of speech and placed a number in front if there were multiple definitions. It was actually kind of funny.

"Very good, Hank," said Mr. Tillman. "Now, put the definition in your own words. I know you can read, but I want to know if you can think."

"Well, it means that this horse might as well have three legs or no legs at all, because he can never win a race."

"Anyone else?" asked Mr. Tillman.

"It's like people who lose so much and so often they get tired of trying. They just say forget it. Why keep trying?" Sheila said.

"Well, if you do not try you are guaranteed to lose," said Marvin.

Everybody was surprised because this was the first time Marvin spoke since returning to school after being bullied.

"It's like if I did not come back to school others would have won, but I decided to get back up and try again. If I would have stayed home I would have been that word on the board. What is it?"

"Everybody say *also-ran*," said Mr. Tillman.

"Also-ran."

"Also-ran, to be, or not to be—that is the question," said Mr. Tillman.

Kenny raised his hand.

"Go ahead, Kenny."

"It's like this movie I was watching about a civil rights preacher in Birmingham, Alabama, and everybody wanted him to stop preaching sermons because they were afraid that it would get the segregationists angry."

"Word wall, word wall!" Our class called this out whenever someone used one of the words from our standing-tall word wall.

"Back to what I was saying. This preacher decided it was time to stand up for what he believed in even when his own people were trying to keep him quiet. They even threatened to remove him from the church. But he just kept on fighting because he believed it was the right thing to do."

"How are you connecting that to *also-ran*?" asked Mr. Tillman.

"Well, if he believed that he was going to lose the battle, he would have stopped fighting."

"Very good, Kenny," said Mr. Tillman. "Let's get a bit more personal. Is the spirit of the also-ran among us?"

"Yep," I said. "People give up all the time. Some people have just stopped trying. Even in this class."

"What do you mean?" asked Mr. Tillman.

"If we really tried hard, we wouldn't be in the predicament we are in right now."

"Word wall, word wall!"

"Speak for yourself," said Alex.

"Y'all know I am right. If we tried harder we wouldn't have so many people in this school failing. Before this year, most of us didn't even read a book, and we sure didn't know most of those words on the wall."

"I did," said Alex.

"Most of us couldn't write the pledge. Remember that. We were acting like a whole bunch of also-rans, teachers included. Some of our parents, too."

Mr. Tillman started singing. "Wade in the water. Wade in the water, children. Wade in the water, God's a-going to trouble the water." He would sometimes break into song to catch our attention and build on our discussion. He was standing near the door with an old-looking copy of *Moby Dick* in his hand. All of his pages were marked up. He had paper clips on some pages. He told us that this book was usually not read by students until they reached high school, but he believed we could understand a line or two by brother author Herman Melville. He told us that his eighth-grade teacher shared a couple of lines with him that he never forgot. He read two lines:

"Ignorance is the parent of fear."

"In fact, I was so afraid of him that I was not game enough just then to address him."

He told us that the also-ran spirit lives on because of those two lines. People stop racing because of ignorance that leads to fear. They haven't learned to win so they become afraid to try. They do not know what winning feels like so they give up.

Also, they do not know how to address *him* when *him* refers to the person inside. They become afraid of *themselves*. They become afraid to enter the race. This is the most dangerous form of race(ism)—not entering the race.

I did not understand most of the stuff he said about the whale in *Moby Dick*, or how he went from talking about horses to talking about whales, but I did understand when he said, "The only way you can guarantee losing a race is by not entering the race." He told us that that was the only race(ism) that matters.

Half of the eighth-grade year is gone, but I think for the first time in my life, I started believing that I could become somebody special. I am not going to be afraid anymore.

After reading the whole novel, one young African American male handed me the following note:

> Dr. Tatum I really enjoy this book. It's kind of what I went through on the south side [of Chicago]. The teachers acted like they didn't care about me. Students always made fun of me. And they always jump me. In some of my classes I was doing mediocre work. And I just felt fine doing average work. Until I move to North East Community. [Now] I never get jumped. The teachers care about my education. People not mean to me. And my grades and confidence is high.

This student found the text enabling. It led him to put into perspective experiences that occurred before he read the text. The student also used language from the novel—*mediocre*—to explain a situation. Like all the students during my visit, this student was fully engaged with a text that resonated and provided a potential road map for acting in the world.

Moving Beyond Disabling Texts

The texts used with African American males attending schools in high-poverty communities are characteristically disabling texts; that is, they ignore these young male's need for a plan of action, a road map, and a healthy psyche. A disabling text reinforces a student's perception of being a struggling reader incapable of handling cognitively challenging texts. The texts most African American adolescent males receive in school and other settings lack the strong content that will cause them to take action in their own lives. Also, many teachers have a difficult time discussing potentially enabling texts because they are worried about meeting the needs of struggling readers and working texts written years ago into students' modern-day contexts.

For example, let's say I'm required to teach Elie Wiesel's *Night* (1958) in a tenth-grade English classroom to students who may have never read a novel and who dislike reading in general. I'll need to address many challenges regarding excerpts like the following:

> "Why do you cry when you pray?" he asked, as though he knew me well.
>
> "I don't know," I answered, troubled.
>
> I had never asked myself that question. I cried because . . . because something inside me felt the need to cry. That was all I knew.
>
> "Why do you pray?" he asked after a moment.
>
> Why do I pray? Strange question. Why did I live? Why did I breathe?
>
> "I don't know," I told him, even more troubled and ill at ease. "I don't know."
>
> From that day on, I saw him often. He explained to me, with great emphasis, that every question possessed a power that was lost in the answer. . . .
>
> Man comes closer to God through the questions he asks Him, he liked to say. Therein lies true dialogue. Man asks and God replies. But we don't understand His replies. We cannot understand them. Because they dwell in the depths of our souls and remain there until we die. The real answers, Eliezer, you will find only within yourself. (4–5)

If required to use this text, I would begin on page 4 in order to establish momentum, and return to the first page of the text later. It is important to engage adolescents right away and minimize unnecessary digressions that often surface during extensive teacher talk. This excerpt also has a built-in essential question: *what dwells in the depths of our soul and remains there until we die?*

However, creating momentum and asking a question that can lead to an engaging discussion does not address the students' limited reading ability. To do that, I have to identify students' reading-related needs, provide explicit instruction related to those needs, and quite possibly change the conditions of the text. Ultimately, I have to assess their ability to handle text independently.

Let's assume for the moment that I determine that the students are not monitoring their comprehension while reading. This is evident when students read words that do not make sense in context and rarely make self-corrections. For example, a student might read the first sentence of the excerpt as, "'Why do you cry when you *pry?*' he asked, as *though* he knew me well," without realizing that the sentence does not make sense. In that case, I would need to provide explicit strategy instruction and give them opportunities to monitor their comprehension until I am convinced, through ongoing observation and assessment, that the students understand what they are reading.

One way I could approach this is to inform the students that good readers monitor their comprehension while reading—they pay attention to their own reading to determine if it makes sense. I would have them practice with the following paragraphs, inserting words in the blanks that make sense.

> From that day on, I saw him often. He explained to me, with great emphasis, that every question possessed a power that was lost in the answer. . . .
>
> Man comes _____ to God through the questions he asks Him, he liked to say. Therein lies true dialogue. Man _____ and God replies. But we don't understand His replies. We cannot _____ them. Because they dwell in the depths of our souls and _____ there until we die. The real answers, Eliezer, you will find only within yourself.

The goal is not for students to match the author's words exactly, but to construct meaning by paying close attention to the text. The following would be accepted:

> Man comes <u>nearer</u> to God through the questions he asks Him, he liked to say. Therein lies true dialogue. Man <u>seeks</u> and God replies. But we don't understand His replies. We cannot <u>realize</u> them. Because they dwell in the depths of our souls and <u>stay</u> there until we die. The real answers, Eliezer, you will find only within yourself.

(Appendix A is another example of explicit instruction I have used with high school students who struggled with reading.)

Many teachers struggling to meet the needs of low-achieving readers select texts based on their students' reading-related needs and ignore their need for human development. To my dismay, I observed one of my graduate students, during her first week in a reading clinic, select *The Berenstain Bears* (a book for primary students) to use with a sixteen-year-old African American male. Why would a well-intentioned tutor attending an urban institution of higher education place this developmentally appropriate but *disabling* text in front of a high school student? Focusing on improving his reading without regard to the content of the text limited and weakened her instruction.

African American adolescent males need texts that speak to the power of the individual and the power of the collective, allowing many of them to hear their own inner voices for the first time ever and move beyond a "cult of victimology" (McWhorter 2006). Texts must allow these young males to enter a space previously undiscovered because it is cobwebbed, masked, or sealed off by darkness, so that they become deep thinkers about the past, present, and future.

Such a text is Ayi Kwei Armah's *Two Thousand Seasons* (1973/2000). The excerpts below can be used to help African American males examine their origins and realize how the annihilation of thought about their origins contributes to their being accomplices to their own destruction (as suggested by some of their actions). Additionally they can be used to nurture the appreciation of gorgeous writing; each is essential.

> A people losing sight of origins are dead. A people deaf to purposes are lost. Under fertile rain, in scorching sunshine, there is no difference: their bodies are mere corpses, awaiting final burial. (xv)

> Completely ruined, bled of life's juices, they have staggered groping for the source, their purpose now the condemned past. Unable to stagger further, they lie unburied by the common road, their corpses multiplying, their feet pointing to their destruction. (xviii)

Powerful texts like this can move these young men beyond a virginal state of literacy development. Once they read a powerful book, powerful essay, or powerful poem that sparks their humanity, they can never return to a place or stance of unknowing with regard to the power found in words and how words can awaken the human spirit. In time, they will begin to trust texts. Texts must be audited and selected that will tap into their feelings, imagination, and intellectual curiosity. The following excerpt from Richard Wright's *Black Boy* (1945) describes the narrator's response to a story:

> She whispered to me the story of Bluebeard and His Seven Wives and I ceased to see the porch, the sunshine, her face, everything. As her words fell upon my new ears, I endowed them with a reality that welled up from somewhere within me. . . . The tale made the world around me be, throb, live. As she spoke, reality changed, the look of things altered, and the world became peopled with magical presences. My sense of life deep-

ened and the feel of things was different, somehow. . . . The sensations of the story aroused in me were never to leave me. (45)

William Lloyd Garrison, a white abolitionist, understood this when he began editing and publishing *The Liberator,* an antislavery newspaper. Using some of the language of the Declaration of Independence, he introduced the first edition of the newspaper with strong language aimed at tapping into the degradation experienced by blacks:

Assenting to the "self-evident truth" maintained in the American Declaration of Independence, "that all men are created equal, and endowed by their Creator with certain unalienable rights—among which are life, liberty, and the pursuit of happiness," I shall strenuously contend for the immediate enfranchisement of our slave population. (1)

Black subscribers enthusiastically supported *The Liberator.* It became an enabling text for many in the fight to abolish slavery in the United States.

The Bible, the Declaration of Independence, Walker's *Appeal, The Liberator,* and *Narrative of the Life of Frederick Douglass, An American Slave* (Douglass 1845) were enabling texts for black males who could read in the early and mid-nineteenth century. These enabling texts became central to their development because they found them to be meaningful and significant to their lives. These and other texts led them to think deeply about their existence.

As a young man, Frederick Douglass' imagination was set on fire by *The Columbian Orator* (Blight 1998), a text that contributed to his human transformation. Douglas Miller, in *Frederick Douglass and the Fight for Freedom* (1988), writes:

At the age of 13, Frederick, having earned 50 cents shining shoes, bought his first book, a secondhand copy of a widely used school text called *The Columbian Orator.* The book consisted of short speeches by renowned orators praising temperance, honesty, courage, diligence, liberty, freedom, equality, and democracy. There were addresses by such famous people as George Washington, Cicero, Socrates, Charles Fox, and William Pitt. Frederick read their eloquent words over and over. He was particularly impressed by Daniel O'Connor's moving appeal for Catholic emancipation in Ireland. He interpreted this as "a bold denunciation of slavery, and a powerful vindication of human rights."

The book also contained bits of dialogue for students to memorize. One of these was an exchange between a master and a slave in which the slave finally convinced the master of the immorality of slavery and his duty to set him free. The more Frederick read the book, the more he detested slavery. He now regarded slaveholders as a band of successful robbers, who had left their homes, and gone to Africa, and stolen us from our homes, and in this strange land reduced us to slavery.

The Columbian Orator confirmed Frederick's belief in human equality, but it also deepened his discontent. He was still a slave. The book had given him a view of his wretched condition, without a remedy: "It opened my eyes to the horrible pit, but no ladder upon which to get out." So great was his despair that he almost envied other slaves their ignorance. (14–15)

Douglass' words, "[The book] opened my eyes . . ." highlight the enabling characteristics of texts. The book confirmed Douglass' belief in human equality; the book had given him a view of his wretched condition; and as a result of his reading, he now regarded slaveholders as a band of successful robbers.

The *Columbian Orator* shaped Douglass' trajectory toward becoming an abolitionist. "The readings of these documents *enable me* to utter my thoughts and to meet the arguments brought forward to sustain slavery" (Douglass 1845/1997, 54). Still unable to write well and not having a full understanding of the word *abolitionist*, young Douglass challenged his enslaver as a result of his reading. The text moved him to act on his own life. Below is a section of the dialogue between slave and master that he memorized from *The Columbian Orator*.

MAST: NOW, villain! What have you to say for this second attempt to run away? Is there any punishment that you do not deserve?

SLAVE: I well know that nothing I can say will avail. I submit to my fate.

MAST: But are you not a base fellow, a hardened and ungrateful rascal?

SLAVE: I am a slave. That is answer enough.

MAST: I am not content with that answer. I thought I discerned in you some tokens of a mind superior to your condition. I treat you accordingly. You have been comfortably fed and lodged, not overworked, and attended with the most humane care when you were sick. And is this the return?

SLAVE: Since you condescended to talk with me, as man to man, I will reply. What have you done, what can you do for me, that will compensate for the liberty which you have taken away?

MAST: I did not take it away. You were a slave when I fairly purchased you.

SLAVE: Did I give my consent to the purchase?

MAST: You had no consent to give. You had already lost the right of disposing yourself.

SLAVE: I had lost the power, but how the right? I was treacherously kidnapped in my own country, when following an honest occupation. I was put in chains, sold to one of your countrymen, carried by force aboard his ship, brought hither, and exposed to the sale like a beast in a market, where you bought me. What step in all this progress of violence and injustice can give a *right*? Was it in the villain who stole me, in the slave-merchant who tempted him to do so, or in you who encouraged the slave-merchant to bring his cargo to cultivate your lands?

MAST: It is the order of Providence that one man should become subservient to another. It ever has been so, and ever will be. I found the custom, and did not make it.

SLAVE: You cannot but be sensible, that the robber who puts a pistol to your breast may make just the same plea. Providence gives him power over your life and property; it gave my enemies a power over my liberty. But it has also given me legs to escape with; and what should prevent me from using them? Nay, what should restrain me from retaliating wrongs I have suffered, if a favourable occasion should offer? (209–210)

This powerful enabling text shattered Douglass' contentedness with his present condition. It should become clear why he confronted his enslaver, escaped to freedom, and worked on behalf of his enslaved brethren and his and their posterity. His psyche changed as a result of his reading this text. He became someone different.

I often found myself regretting my own existence, and wishing myself dead; and but for the hope of being free, I have no doubt I would have killed myself, or done something for which I should have been killed. While in this state of mind I was eager to hear any one speak of slavery. I was a ready listener. (1845/1997, 55)

Enabling Texts in the Mid-Twentieth Century

Texts continued to enable African American males throughout the twentieth century. The effects of these enabling texts were particularly prevalent during the 1960s and 1970s, as reflected in many autobiographical and biographical narratives written during these two decades. Some well-known narratives, many of them written by authors who developed postprison literacy, are:

The Autobiography of Malcolm X, by Alex Haley and Malcolm X (1965)
Soul on Ice, by Eldridge Cleaver (1968)
Die Nigger Die! by H. Rap Brown (1969/2002)
Soledad Brother: The Prison Letters of George Jackson (1970)

The relationship of these texts to and their impact on African American males is captured clearly by George Jackson in *Blood in My Eye* (1972/1990):

> I met Marx, Lenin, Trotsky, Engels, and Mao . . . and they *redeemed* [my emphasis] me. For the first four years, I studied nothing but economics and military ideas. I met black guerrillas . . . [and] we attempted to transform the black criminal mentality into a black revolutionary mentality. (xi)

Jackson refers to Lenin's *The State and Revolution* (1918/1992) and "how revolution is an imperative, a love-inspired, conscious act of desperation" (9) and "how each popular struggle must be analyzed historically to discover new ideas" (13). He also describes the real reason for reading and the intended impact of books: "This means that after we are done with books, they must be put aside; and the search for method will depend on observation, correct analysis, creativity and seizing the time" (23). Jackson entered prison as an eighteen-year-old for committing a robbery, but he became a "world-connected citizen" living within a prison cell because of texts. He was transformed. "[He] was captured and brought to prison when [he] was 18 years old because [he] couldn't adjust" (Jackson 1970, 4), and yet he used this time to transform himself through texts.

In a similar vein, Cleaver (1968) writes how he concentrated his reading in the field of economics and sought out books about Marx because everyone was condemning him. "Although he kept me with a headache, I took [Marx] as my authority" (31). Admittedly he read several texts with very little understanding, but he sought to incorporate the readings into his own behavior:

I began consciously incorporating these principles into my daily life, to employ tactics of ruthlessness in my dealings with everyone with whom I came into contact. And I began to look at white America through these new eyes. (31)

Ultimately, Cleaver was moved to write because of his reading:

I started to write to save myself. I realized that no one could save me but myself. The prison authorities were both uninterested and unable to help me. I had to seek truth and unravel the snarled web of my motivations. I had to find out who I am and what I want to be, what type of man I should be, and what I can do to become the best of which I was capable. I understood that what happened to me had also happened to countless other blacks and it would happen to many, many more. (34)

During the 1960s and 1970s, several well-known and highly referenced enabling texts figured prominently in the literacy development of African American males engaged in the struggle to demand their civil and God-given rights while living under America's umbrella of oppressive hatred. Frantz Fanon's *The Wretched of the Earth* (1963) and *Black Skin, White Masks* (1967) were two of these texts. "Every brother on the rooftop could quote Brother Fanon" (Van Deburg 1992). In *Black Skin, White Masks* Fanon writes about the fact of blackness and how the colonized men of color became broken by how they were perceived by others. He provides an enabling message that is as relevant for African Americans today as it was when it was written forty years ago:

The crippled veteran of the Pacific war says to my brother, "Resign yourself to your color the way I got used to my stump; we're both victims." Nevertheless with all my strength I refuse to accept that amputation, I feel in myself a soul as immense as the world, truly a soul as deep as the deepest of rivers, my chest has the power to expand without limit. I am a master and I am advised to adopt the humility of the cripple. (140)

This text is very similar to "Invictus," by William Henley, which I read and memorized during my eighth-grade days in the early 1980s. The last lines—*I am the master of my fate: I am the captain of my soul*—hold the same meaning as Fanon's text—*my chest has the power to expand without limit.* Both can be interpreted to mean that the destiny of African American males ultimately rests in the hands of African American males without constraint. This belief and potential reality is one of the outgrowths of reading enabling texts and building a lineage of such texts as one develops and matures.

A Quick Look at Textual Lineages

Several texts repeatedly appear as part of the textual lineages of literate African American males throughout the generations. Figure 4.1 is a summary of the texts I have identified in my study of autobiographical and biographical narratives. It is impractical to list every text that has impacted an African American male; members of this ethnic group are widely diverse, and they are impacted in different ways depending on their personal context. Instead, I list the texts that recurred most frequently.

Texts written by women and canonical texts are glaringly omitted, although both have had a profound effect on many African American males. Carl Upchurch, for example, in *Convicted in the Womb* (1996), writes how Shakespeare's Sonnet 29 transformed him:

> My real connection with Shakespeare started with the line in Sonnet 29: "Like to the lark at the break of day arising." That sonnet, which became my favorite, was about me and my experience, as if Bill [note the familiar shortened form] had just sat down and looked into my heart. (83)

I share this example because high school English teachers often ask if African American adolescent males should read Shakespeare or other canonical texts or just read texts that relate to them. This is a misguided, thoughtless question. Students should read texts that have enabling characteristics for them that go beyond being able to say, "I read it for the sake of reading it," or because it is part of the canon or because it will appear on the syllabus of a college English seminar. Upchurch was impacted by Shakespeare's sonnet because it led him to look within. Reading the sonnet was less about Shakespeare's survival than it was about his own. The advocacy must be properly situated. Upchurch helps us think about the potential impact of texts on one's life:

> The literature taught me how to look at myself. It told me regardless of my condition, regardless of the circumstances I came from, I was a legitimate human being and a child of God. But I also learned that society considered me inferior because of my color—and considered any rights and

MID TO LATE 19th CENTURY	EARLY 20th CENTURY	MID 20th CENTURY	LATE 20th CENTURY	EARLY 21st CENTURY
The Bible ————————————————————————————→				
	Up from Slavery ————————————————→			
The Declaration of Independence				
	Souls of Black Folk ————————————→			
Narrative of the Life of Frederick Douglass ——————————————————————————————————————→				
		The Wretched of the Earth		
Appeal to the Coloured Citizens of the World	*The Mis-Education of the Negro* —————————————————→			
		Black Skin, White Masks		
The Liberator		Soul on Ice		
Uncle Tom's Cabin		Die Nigger Die!		
		The Autobiography of Malcolm X ————————————————————————→		
		Native Son ————→		
		Black Boy ————————————→		
		Invisible Man ————→		
		Stolen Legacy		
		They Came Before Columbus		
		Message to the Black Man		
		Go Tell It on the Mountain		
		The State and the Revolution		
		Das Kapital		
		Guerilla Warfare		
		The Selected Works of Mao Tse-tung		

The arrows indicate that texts were mentioned as part of males' textual lineages across decades in the document study I conducted. The wide readership of several of the texts was central to specific decades.

Fig. 4.1: *Enabling Texts Through the Decades*

privileges I have as a black man to be the gift of white men. I decided I couldn't respect a process that had to legislate me into being. I also decided I had a responsibility to stand up for people who hadn't yet learned to think of themselves as human beings. (92)

Our current president, Barack Obama, also credits a textual lineage. An article written for the *New York Times* by Kakutani (2009) during the campaign says

[President] Obama's first book, *Dreams From My Father*, . . . suggests that throughout his life he has turned to books as a way of acquiring insights and information from others—as a means of breaking out of the bubble of selfhood. . . . He recalls that he read James Baldwin, Ralph Ellison, Langston Hughes, Richard Wright, and W. E. B. Du Bois when he was an adolescent in an effort to come to terms with his racial identity. . . . As a boy growing up in Indonesia, [President] Obama learned about the American civil rights movement through books his mother gave him. Later . . . he found inspiration in *Parting the Waters*, the first installment of Taylor Branch's multivolume biography of the Rev. Dr. Martin Luther King Jr.

Using the texts in the figure I identified four characteristics that African American males found significant and meaningful.

1. The texts promoted a healthy psyche.

2. They reflected an awareness of the real world.

3. They focused on the collective struggle of African Americans.

4. They served as a road map for being, doing, thinking, and acting.

These characteristics have implications for selecting and mediating enabling texts with African American adolescent males in the twenty-first century.

The Severing of Texts

Texts that African American males can identify as central to their development and thinking (or texts with qualities that have enabled them) have been severed and severely compromised during the middle and late twentieth century because there is a tendency to expose these young males to fewer texts in schools—and because the existing literacy paradigm in U.S. schools focuses on reading scores and has produced a testing frenzy. Three years ago, I began to ask African American males in middle and high school to construct their textual lineage (see the form in Figure 4.2) to determine if they were reading texts that they find meaningful and significant—texts that they thought they would always remember. During 2006–2007, I collected 243 textual lineages of African American adolescent boys. On average, the boys identified 2.7 books on their textual lineages. However, the African American adolescent males reading below grade level and assigned to lower-level reading tracks averaged 0.6 texts in their textual lineage. A sampling of the books in these textual lineages, and the comments the boys included, is provided in Figure 4.3.

Productive Starting Points for Strengthening Our Educational Ideology

1. Examine texts for characteristics that will enable African American adolescent males; these texts should be anchored by a clear definition of the role of literacy development.

2. Identify texts that may be a radical departure from what is currently being offered to economically disadvantaged African American adolescent males attending today's middle and high schools (and other social and educational institutions).

3. Select texts that awaken the consciousness and advance the literacy development of these young men.

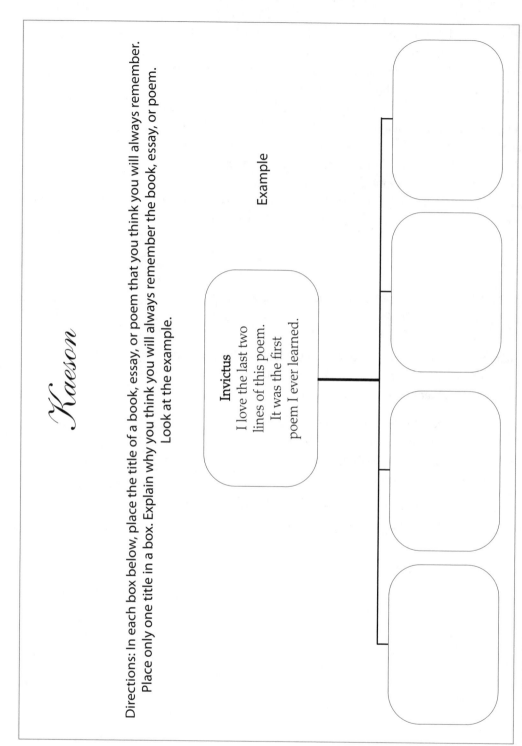

Kaeson

Directions: In each box below, place the title of a book, essay, or poem that you think you will always remember. Place only one title in a box. Explain why you think you will always remember the book, essay, or poem. Look at the example.

Example

Invictus
I love the last two lines of this poem. It was the first poem I ever learned.

Fig. 4.2: *Middle School Student's Textual Lineage*

TEXTS	COMMENTS
Bronx Masquerade	It showed how everyone doesn't have a perfect life, and *it showed that you have to pick life decisions wisely.*
A Raisin in the Sun	I like that story because it shows everything that some families go through, and *it teaches you to stand up for your rights.*
The Odyssey	I liked it because it's just like life. It has lots of obsticles you have to go through in order to make it in life.
"Test of a Man"	I liked this one poem because it proves whether you're a man or if you are still a child. In other words, it separates the boys from the men.
Forged by Fire	*This gave me an idea* to always look after my younger siblings.
Smoked	This book will always remind me of how the life you have is very valuable, and *don't waste it doing wrong things.*
The Bible	Inspiring and *it gives me help on deciding how to live my life.*
Black Boy	First book that *make me feel connected* to African American struggle.
Kaffir Boy	It was an intense book about how Africans were treated during the Apartheid. It *was eye opening* to things that are happening around the world.
Nowhere to Call Home	It's a good book and *made me think about life.*
Tears of a Tiger	It was the book that really changed my attitude, and I really like it.
The Color of Water	The *book speaks to me as I am trying to find myself,* but it seems to always involve finding my mother.
Keys to Free Your Mind	This *book enlightened my thinking* by reinforcing the ideas I already know. It was uplifting reading them in a book knowing that my brain works like other people. I read this like a writer.
We Real Cool	It reminds me of the way life is.
To Kill a Mockingbird	Because *it had a big impact on the way I viewed* the civil rights era.
I forgot the title but it's the auto-biography of Frederick Douglass	I thought it was amazing how one person with nothing but self-determination could change his life around.
Number the Stars	This was a good book that *taught me not to take life for granted.*
Soul on Ice	Dude used to smoke weed, he went to jail, then he changed his life around.
Gifted Hands	This book *helped me realize* that no matter how bad things are, just have a little faith and try your hardest and you will always prevail.
Up from Slavery	This book was very inspirational, and *it gave me hope and helped me build my self-esteem.*

Fig. 4.3: *Texts and Comments from the Lineages of African American Adolescent Males*

Ideology

by Alfred W. Tatum

You know,
it strikes me,
there is no ideology
when it comes to educating me.
You would rather I read Shakespeare for the sake of Shakespeare's survival
Not my own.
I want to survive too.
Shakespeare and I can co-exist if you insist,
But help me understand that I exist in this co-existence.
Fight for my right.
After all, I am still alive.
Shakespeare is dead—you know that, right?
I am not sure if he even cared about me the way you want me to care for him.
Will he help me get off the block?
I have not been convinced that he is the answer, in part or fully, to the social
    ills plaguing young black brothers.
But I will read *Antigone* if you give me a chance and show me how.
I care about love.
But I want to be loved too.
It's hard to read about love in a loveless environment.
I don't care who is writing.
Your imprints upon my psyche are just as real as the imprints on the page.
I can't pay attention to one while you expect me to ignore the other.
When it comes to educating me
Strengthen the Ideology.
The next time someone wants to water down the curriculum and have me
    read some bullshit
Stand on top of the table and shout—Hell No!
Let them know I am someone's child.
When it comes to educating me
Strengthen the Ideology.
Three final phrases to help you in this plight
Fight for my right to Be!
Fight for my right to Be!
Fight for my right to Be!
Just fight for me—every time I fight I seem to get in trouble.
Fight for me—shape a positive trajectory—please!
    Ahhhhhh, Shakespeare!

Choosing, Creating, and Mediating Enabling Texts

That future was so clear to us—our generation could not escape the destiny of marching down to terminate the racial insult that rebuked our very being as blacks. Whenever I had cause to think of that prospect, I confess that I felt nothing but a warm glow of anticipation.

—WOLE SOYINKA

He has not mastered London. If there is any mastering going on, it is London mastering him.

—J. M. COETZEE

■ **Essential question for students and educators:** Why establish a relationship with text?

In this chapter, I bring attention to choosing, creating, and mediating enabling texts. I also bring attention to ways to stimulate students' engagement while avoiding nonproductive trappings that can potentially serve as barriers to students' engagement. Four platforms for choosing, creating, and mediating texts will be introduced. Additionally, I offer several considerations for addressing some of the tensions that exist for teachers when charged with mediating texts across culture and gender.

James Baldwin, in his intellectually gritty, often messy rebuttals to society's attempts to define him and his lyric efforts to define himself, is a must-read writer for African American adolescent males—primarily because his essays are a model for expressing identity shaped by complex contexts. He chooses powerful words in which are embedded trenchant messages about the meaning of self. Baldwin had this to say after reading *Uncle Tom's Cabin*:

> Slowly I discovered that according to society, I was a *nigger*. It was hard to accept and I decided to refuse! I decided that whatever I did wouldn't be on society's terms but on my own. I would do anything to survive; they would have to hear from me. . . . I felt a rage like fever, and I learned that you have to find a way of living with it or you just have to surrender to it. I wasn't going to surrender to anything or anybody. (Weatherby 1977, 14)

There is a connection between Baldwin's words and those of J. M. Coetzee (2002)—winner of the Nobel Prize in literature—in *Youth*, a memoir in the guise of a novel that provides glimpses into the life of a young man trying to find his way in the world. The young man moves from South Africa to London but still finds that his world and his thinking—more pointedly his writing—is funneled through a South African experience he wants to leave behind. Coetzee writes:

> It disquiets him to see that he is still writing about South Africa. He would prefer to leave his South African self behind as he has left South Africa itself behind. South Africa was a bad start, a handicap. An undistinguished, rural family, bad schooling, the Afrikaans language: from each of these component handicaps he has, more or less, escaped. (62)

Environments can master individuals unless the individuals master their environments— become the master of their fate and the captain of their soul, to echo William Henley's "Invictus."

Avoiding Caricatures

Texts saturated with African American male caricatures and unconnected to other texts can fuel African American adolescent males' belief that they are being mastered by their environment. These caricatures are of two types. One type includes the hoopster, the fatherless son, the gang recruit, the truant, the dummy in need of remediation, and the purveyor of poor grammar. The other type includes the African American male who is scorned for being smart, the one who is trying to break from the norms of his impoverished community, or the one who has beaten the odds and "made it."

Educators and publishers crank out texts featuring these caricatured protagonists in an attempt to get African American adolescent males to read, without thoughtfully considering what aspects of texts prompt real engagement and why. This is an essentialist notion based on the assumption that the texts can do all the work—that teachers do not have to examine their legitimacy, authenticity, and momentum. Ultimately text selection has to be guided by a deeply purposeful understanding of students' personal, cultural, sexual, communal, national, and international contexts—and a desire to shape these contexts without apology.

Texts with language that is at odds with contemporary African American males' experience (or which diminishes that experience) will turn them off. I am not suggesting that texts outside the realm of students' immediate experiences should be avoided. I *am* suggesting that potential roadblocks—language, content, significance—should be considered. Engaging students initially involves connecting the text to something they can immediately wrap their minds around.

In the summer of 2008 I was working with twelve African American adolescent males. In one discussion, a fourteen-year-old boy mentioned that reading and writing had no benefit in the area in which he lived. I was struck by the phrase he used—*not in my neighborhood*—and wrote the following *black short* (a name we gave to short stories *by* and *for* African American teenage males) to model for these young men how they must live with their eyes, ears, and hearts open and how they must be ready to put their voice on record. The short story was also written to stimulate engaging dialogue among the young men, dialogue that extends beyond the story.

"Not in My Neighborhood"
by Alfred W. Tatum

Trey's bright red cap, half-cocked, was the first thing I noticed when he entered the room. I wasn't sure why he'd showed up, but something about his presence was welcome. His movements were slow and measured. I could hear the questions he was asking, although he remained silent. The baby face atop the grown-man frame was weathered with pain but not totally washed of innocence. He was teetering between things that were difficult to pinpoint. Then he spoke. "Not in my neighborhood."

"Bull crap," I said. "Do something about it."

"Man, all of this is bull crap. We are sitting around waving our pens like magic wands, but we can't write anything that's going to change anything."

Struck by his halting, troubling words, I had to find a way to reconcile myself to the young man's truth without abandoning my own. He had been stunted by a reality I did not fully understand (although images abounded in the media), but his sense of gloom warranted a serious yet careful conversation. I needed to keep him talking.

Trey preferred to let his body do the talking—arms folded across his chest, a grimace covering his inability to understand, sitting silently slumped in his chair. Each stance spoke volumes, marking him as different, guarded. But hope lay in his presence. The others ignored him as they wrestled with their own personal demons, but he was a distinct patch in the quilt. Not more outstanding, but stitched differently.

"So what is the answer?" I asked.

"I don't have the answer. Nobody has an answer." He shifted in his chair at the table in the middle of the room. His hands were now folded on the rim.

The others stared in anticipation, waiting for a response I had not yet formulated. The work we'd done so far could be destroyed by poorly chosen words or an ideologically foolish explanation that positioned me as an outsider to their day-to-day reality. Did I truly understand? The sands of self-assurance were being washed away by this young man's strong language, softly spoken. I had a few seconds to think, to respond, to question, to recover. It was my move.

"There is a passage in the Bible that says—"

"I don't understand a word in the Bible, please don't go there."

Trey leaned back again, and I felt suffocated by disillusionment. Out of the corner of my eye, I saw two other young men nod in agreement. I had missed the mark. I imagined him asking, *where was the Bible when my friend Jimmy needed it?* Or saying, *I don't know if you know this, but it's not the Bible that people are carrying around that is causing havoc.* The wedge between us was growing wider. It was my move again. Had I lost the only chance I might ever have? It was close to noon; our time together today was about to end. I offered a silent prayer: "Jesus, please guide my words and my thoughts. In your name I pray, amen."

"What is the truth?" I asked.

"It don't exist."

"Is it true that you should just roll over and die? Because the truth is, you are going to die anyway, and there's nothing you can do to stop it."

"Maybe I should."

"Maybe you should."

Totally confused about where this conversation was going, I turned my back to the room of young boys and walked toward the chalkboard. My thoughts were marinating, not yet cooked. The resignation in the young boy's tone was peppered with resistance, and I knew I had him where I wanted him. He was debating my clever questions. I was winning. He did not want to die, and I knew it. Something about death is too final for a young boy and causes him to reject it, to fear it. Where is the chalk, I thought? Searching for it gave me a few more seconds to think. The academic exercise ended abruptly. I heard Trey say, "Write something to stop this." I turned around and saw him holding a gun to Craig's head, his left hand around the other boy's neck. "Let me see what you are going to write on the board now. How are you going to use writing to stop me from pulling the trigger?"

I froze.

"Like I said, not in my neighborhood." He turned and left.

I stared at the frightened faces of the other boys and thought, *maybe Trey is right*. Craig came to the front of the room, picked up the chalk I was searching for and wrote five words on the board. "This is what you should have written," he said.

Establishing Platforms for Literacy Development

The short story above was written as part of my developing work that focuses on creating and using texts to counter roadblocks to engagement by paying attention to four literacy platforms, platforms that generate an excitement for the present and the future. Texts that encompass the four literacy platforms encourage the reader to do a number of things.

1. *Define self*—find the text and language that helps you put your voice on record without waiting for others to define you and your generation.

2. *Become resilient*—remain steadfast in the face of vulnerability occasioned by conditions inside and outside school.

3. *Engage others*—inspire your contemporaries to strive toward better humanity for all.

4. *Build capacity*—create a foundation on which future generations can build their agendas.

These platforms emerged from an investigation of the historical roles texts played in the lives of African American males. For example, Chris Gardner, in *The Pursuit of Happyness* (2006), writes, "By 1970, at age sixteen, a junior already, I honestly didn't think I could survive the roller coaster anymore. . . . School was no longer the haven it had once been" (108). Later, he was kicked off the football team by a coach who found his caustic attitude unacceptable and had found "contraband" in Chris' locker. In Chris' own words, "The contraband? Books. To be more precise: *Die, Nigger, Die!*; *Soul on Ice*; and *The Autobiography of Malcolm X*" (109). This experience

> ended any taste I had for athletics. That combined with my continuing activism, my new observations about the gaps between the haves and have-nots, black and white, and the stories I began to hear from the brothers returning from Vietnam fueled a desire to rebel against the status quo even more. Rather than becoming militant, I rebelled by making my own personal statement. (109)

Gardner's "contraband" textual lineage allowed him to accomplish three of the platforms mentioned above—define himself, become resilient, and engage others.

Texts that incite African American adolescent males to action are often not part of the curriculum. These young men should be encouraged to read texts that cause them to examine the academic and social ills that plague their existence and chip away at their complicit behavior. Paul Laurence Dunbar's poem "Frederick Douglass" stresses the importance of using one's voice without apology.

> And he was no soft-tongued apologist;
> He spoke straightforward, fearlessly uncowed;
> The sunlight of his truth dispelled the mist
> and set in bold relief each dark-hued cloud;
> To sin and crime he gave their proper hue,
> And hurled at evil what was evil's due.

The texts used in our schools must give the young black males the language and vision they need to achieve platforms that are both liberating and empowering (although these texts do not necessarily have to be contemporary to be relevant and powerful).

Reconciling Differences

Getting these texts into classrooms will require that educators reconcile their differences with African American adolescent males from communities of turmoil and eliminate the ongoing tension created by age-old traditions of curriculums that were not developed with the current contexts of these young males in mind.

I am often asked to demonstrate, in a model lesson, the power of using enabling texts with African American males. I challenge the limitations of these requests, not because they are unwarranted, but because a single model misses the larger point of capturing what it means to effectively engage students with texts over a period of several years. Using enabling text is not a "performance"; it is a means of teaching literacy that requires hard work to accomplish. I am also on guard against the potential trap of anticipating that these young males are unreachable, which frees teachers from any guilt over their pedagogical shortcomings.

The young males I have worked with have always responded positively, in due time, to the power of the texts and how they are presented. Texts truly matter—just look at the email below.

Mr. Tatum,

I am a GED teacher for the Michigan Department of Corrections. . . . Many of the concepts . . . in your book *Teaching Reading to Black Adolescent Males* are easily used in the prison setting. I have to confess, though, that I struggle with my students. I realize that motivating students in prison is difficult, yet it is vital for them to use education to escape the revolving door of prison life. Although I am a white male from rural Michigan, I have a passion for education, especially where it concerns prisoners. . . . The last two days have been interesting. I tried to discuss Solzhenitsyn with them. Kind of a "brother under the skin" approach. I was met with glazed eyes. Today I read the story of prison privatization from your book to a class. They were on the edge of their seats. To the next class, I read the story of

Dr. Death from South Africa. Again, the glazed eyes of boredom. As you can see, connecting them with their history/identity has been challenging.

Two of this teacher's text selections were met with glazed eyes while one had these same African American males sitting on the edge of their seats. Their interests, very similar to my former eighth graders' interests, were piqued by an article that included this passage:

> The current prison system in the UK is imported from America, one of the few countries with a higher proportion of its population behind bars than the UK. Many of the same companies are involved. These companies are paid per inmate per day so the more people they locked up, the more money they make. Private prisons hold people for longer than state prisons and lobby the government for harsher sentences.

Although this teacher observed differences in engagement with different texts, he went on to ask several questions that ignored the power of enabling texts. These questions focused on the identities of the teacher and the students (in this case, prisoners).

Here are a few questions for you:

1. Is connecting with black males in prison different from connecting with black males on the street?
2. Does being a white male discredit me from connecting them to their past?
3. Prison already emphasizes racial differences. Most of the information blacks get about their history has been twisted into conspiracy theories and black militancy. This can be dangerous in a prison setting. How do I get around this?

These questions are illustrative of the challenges and tensions that exist when teachers are charged with mediating texts across culture and gender.

Mediating Texts Across Culture and Gender

Administrators who inadvertently communicate that teaching students who do not share your cultural heritage or your gender is difficult give teachers license to fail African American adolescent males from communities of turmoil. During a meeting with a superintendent of a southern school district of more than a hundred thousand students I was asked if I could show white female teachers how to present texts to African American adolescent males. This question unfairly indicts white female teachers. We are *all* guilty of failing to advance the literacy development of African American adolescent males by connecting them to the power of texts.

In his book *Blindness*, José Saramago (1997) writes, "to an arrow shot into the air, which upon reaching its highest point, pauses for a moment as if suspended, and then begins to trace its obligatory descending curve" (121). How have we, as educators, failed to see that we are not serving segments of our student population? And what must we do to restore our vision, to reconcile ethnic and gender differences? It is not our skin color that interrupts effective literacy instruction, but how we view the role of literacy instruction in schools.

Policy makers, administrators, and classroom teachers are all shooting metaphoric arrows. What are the limiting forces? Are white female teachers the only ones having difficulty? The answer to the second question is no. Here is my answer to the administrator who asked, "Can you show our white female teachers how to use texts with African American adolescent males?"

Dear Superintendent:

Effectively presenting texts to adolescents, particularly African American adolescent males from communities of turmoil, requires the following:

1. Recognizing that all students have multiple identities—personal, cultural, and gender related.
2. Reconceptualizing literacy instruction to mean more than increasing students' assessment scores.
3. Giving careful consideration to students' in- and out-of-school contexts when evaluating and choosing texts.
4. Paying attention to clearly defined platforms of literacy development.
5. Nurturing zones of negotiation that invite students' voices into the process of learning.
6. Being willing to fail and recover.
7. Providing explicit skill and strategy instruction and providing appropriate models when necessary.
8. Moving beyond the "perceived" limitations/advantages of skin color.

9. Using texts as the mediating variable to strengthen teacher/student and student/student relationships.
10. Exercising patience and resilience.
11. Being ready when they show up.
12. Getting into the text right away and having a consistent routine.
13. Leading challenging text discussions in racially integrated and racially segregated environments.

To be more pointed, let's say your teachers are charged with teaching Albert Camus's *The Rebel* to African American adolescent males, those who struggle with reading and those who do not. These teachers have to determine:

1. Where in the text to begin.
2. How to introduce the text.
3. How to frame the text with questions that the students might find essential.
4. How to connect the texts to larger goals that will give the text a sustaining quality.

I drafted the attached tangible guidelines for constructing essential questions [see Figure 5.1] and submitted it to a group of high school teachers as a starting point for our work together. I hope you will find them useful. I have also designed a framework teachers can use to accomplish these aims when presenting and mediating a text. I attach a blank form [see Figure 5.2], as well as a completed one as an example [see Figure 5.3].

Mediating texts with African American adolescent males requires careful consideration and planning from *all* teachers, not just white female teachers. I have not always been successful on my first attempts, but the framework's guidelines have been extremely useful. I constantly ask myself, *out of all of the texts in the world, why do I want to put this text in front of my students?* Such an audit is critical.

I recently assessed Ji-Li Jiang's *Red Scarf Girl: A Memoir of the Cultural Revolution* (1997) as a text to use with adolescents. It aligns neatly with two of the literacy platforms, engaging others and building capacity, and I decided I could absolutely teach two of the chapters—"Destroy the Four Olds" and "Writing Da-Zi-Bao."

What Is an Essential Question?

⇒ An essential question moves educators and students to engage in dialogue about issues or concepts that matter in school and society.

⇒ An essential question may cause internal conflicts.

⇒ An essential question cannot be settled by one person.

⇒ An essential question can be addressed from multiple perspectives and in relation to multiple identities.

Specific Things to Consider

1. Identify content objectives you would like your students to meet. For example, *I want the students to learn about the apartheid that took place in South Africa before examining other forms of apartheid. Or, I want students to learn about the human genome.*

2. Ask yourself what the larger problems/issues/questions addressed by the texts are. For example, *Kaffir Boy* focuses on a child's experience during South Africa's apartheid era. A larger issue or essential question is, *how does someone construct their visibility in a society that refuses to recognize them? Or, is there a need to balance science and religion?*

3. Think about a question that students can respond to from their multiple perspectives and in terms of their multiple identities. For example, *what does it mean to exist? Or, do we find or create ourselves?*

4. Use an essential question to anchor the significance or "essence" of why you are teaching the text and the additional benefits students can obtain from reading and discussing it. In other words, ask yourself, *why do I want my students to read the text I am selecting out of all of the texts that exist in the world? Why should the students be aware of this text and its contents?*

5. Construct the essential questions with an aim to rescue and refine the significance of teaching and to improve the human condition. For example, *what is the role of teaching in the United States?* is an essential question for high school teachers to answer.

6. Revisit the essential questions throughout the semester and from one semester to the next. An essential question should not relate to one lesson only. Students should be able to revisit it over time. For example, *is a person's life outcome determined by race, gender, or economics? Or, does one's ability determine their life outcome? Or, is the individual in control of their destiny?*

Rationale and Caution

Developing essential questions should help us seriously consider curriculum orientations, the role of literacy instruction, and responsive pedagogy as we implement our instructional strategies. Our educational philosophy and our instructional strategies cannot—or should not—be separated. Fortunately, each of us can decode, read fluently, and monitor our comprehension. We also have a strong concept of reading and a well-developed vocabulary. Additionally, we can construct our own questions to determine what to pay attention to and how to respond to texts. These skills are related to the ability to read and comprehend texts.

The texts we choose to read or ignore are also related to engagement. We cannot leave the reader behind as we focus on essential questions. Shaping students' literacies and their ability to comprehend cognitively challenging texts independently is the ultimate goal. We must find ways to use texts and teach strategies to shape students' positive life outcome trajectories, not become complicit in shaping the life outcome gaps related to low levels of literacy in the United States. All students should be able to chime in, "I too sing America." They won't be able to if we focus on skills and strategies alone. They are limited by an underexposure to texts they find meaningful and significant. Meaning and significance can be nurtured by the essential questions constructed to meet this aim.

Fig. 5.1: *Guidelines for Developing Essential Questions*

Literacy Platforms
- Defining Self _____
- Becoming Resilient _____
- Engaging Others _____
- Building Capacity _____
- Other _____

Introducing the Text (*getting adolescents into the text right away*)
- Required vocabulary—[1 to 3 words]
- Text to introduce the text—use an excerpt to get the students involved right away

Framing Question(s)

Writing Connection (*calling attention to the text as a language model and helping the students read as writers*)

Mediating Discussions Around One of the Framing Questions
Assign pages of text to read. It is best to begin with one page of text and discuss it together before releasing the responsibility to the students in:
1. Small groups.
2. Whole groups.
3. Individual writing assignments.

Evaluating the Discussion and Students' Ongoing Needs in Future Discussions

Fig. 5.2: *Blank Framework for Mediating Text*

Literacy Platforms
- Defining Self __✓__
- Becoming Resilient __✓__
- Engaging Others _____
- Building Capacity _____
- Other _____

Introducing the Text (*getting adolescents into the text right away*)
- Required vocabulary—[*rebellion, integrity*]
- Text to introduce the text—use an excerpt to get the students involved right away

The rebel refuses to allow anyone to touch what he is. He is fighting for the integrity of one part of his being. He does not try, primarily, to conquer, but simply to impose (force his will on others). (p. 18)

Heathcliff, in *Wuthering Heights*, says that he puts his love above God and would willingly go to hell in order to be reunited with the woman he loves. (p. 19)

Rebellion, though apparently negative, since it creates nothing, is profoundly positive in that it reveals that part of man which must always be defended. (p. 19)

Framing Question(s)
- What are the *true* benefits of rebellion?
- What parts of you are you willing to defend at all cost?
- Are there connections between rebellion and defining oneself and becoming resilient (*connects to platforms*)?
- Have we surrendered our right to rebel? In this school? In our community? In our nation?

Writing Connection (*calling attention to the text as a language model and helping the students read as writers*)
Let's examine how the author put the first chapter together. Looking at the three quotes above, what do you think about the author's:
1. Word choice—is he using words to invite the reader in or lock the reader out?
2. Voice—does it sound like a real voice? Is he taking care as an author to get his point across?
3. Momentum—is he able to keep the reader's attention? Why or why not?
4. Investment—does he seem to really care about what he is writing about?

Let's turn to the first paragraph of chapter 1:

What is a rebel? A man who says no, but whose refusal does not imply renunciation. He is also a man who says yes, from the moment he makes his first gesture of rebellion. A slave who has taken orders all of his life suddenly decides that he cannot obey some new command. What does he mean by saying "no"? (p. 13)
What can we say about
1. Word choice—is he using words to invite the reader in or lock the reader out?
2. Voice—does it sound like a real voice? Is he taking care as an author to get his point across?
3. Momentum—is he able to keep the reader's attention? Why or why not?
4. Investment—does he seem to really care about what he is writing about?

continues

Fig. 5.3: *Example of a Completed Framework for Mediating Camus'* The Rebel

Mediating Discussions Around One of the Framing Questions
Assign pages of text to read. It is best to begin with one page of text and discuss it together before releasing the responsibility to the students in:
1. Small groups.
2. Whole groups.
3. Individual writing assignments.

Evaluating the Discussion and Students' Ongoing Needs in Future Discussions
1. Pacing.
2. Grouping.
3. Instructional support and modeling.

Fig. 5.3:   *Continued*

In "Destroy the Four Olds," the author plants seeds for intelligent discussion in these passages:

> Our beloved Chairman Mao had started the Cultural Revolution in May. Every day since then on the radio we heard about the need to end the pernicious influences of the "Four Olds": old ideas, old culture, old customs, and old habits. Chairman Mao told us we would never succeed in building a strong socialist country until we destroyed the "Four Olds" and established the "Four News." (21)

> The rotten ideas and customs we were used to, were inside ourselves. (28)

In the chapter, students were challenged to "go home and thoroughly remold [their] ideology" (33).

"Writing Da-Zi-Bao," although written within an international context that differs from ours in the United States, can be used to critique our educational system.

> Who would have believed that our entire educational system was wrong after all? Seventeen years after Liberation, the newspapers told us, our schools were not bringing up good red socialists and communists, as we had thought, but revisionists. We thanked heaven that Chairman Mao

had started this Cultural Revolution, and that the Central Committee of the Communist Party had uncovered the mess in our schools. Otherwise we would not have even known that we were in trouble. What a frightening idea! (38)

A few pages later the author writes:

Although teachers do not hold bombs or knives, they are still dangerous enemies. They fill us with insidious revisionist ideas. They teach us that scholars are superior to workers. They promote personal ambition by encouraging competition for the highest grades. All these things are intended to change good young socialists into corrupt revisionists. They are invisible knives that are even more dangerous than real knives or guns. (41)

Connecting *Red Scarf Girl* to *The Rebel* prompts a fluid conversation about rebellion, resistance, reimagining, and reconciling oneself to existing possibilities. Both have the potential to become a part of students' textual lineages if mediated effectively; both can be enabling texts. The constant challenge is finding enabling texts that can serve as links between teachers and students within cultures and across cultures. An examination of texts written by African American male authors will lead to the realization that African American males living in the United States have had to reconcile their identity with what it means to live in this strange land, and many are in constant negotiation with the American context. If the goal of literacy instruction is to shape positive life trajectories, then we must shoot different arrows—different texts. I argue that it doesn't matter who is shooting the arrows; the types of arrows being shot matters more.

Productive Starting Points

1. Use the framework for mediating text with a short literary or nonliterary selection. Gauge the students' reactions. Reflect on the lesson and student response to help you plan subsequent lessons. Don't let the framework take over the text. Ultimately, it's the texts that matter, particularly if the selection of the texts is guided by something deeply purposeful.

2. Help students build a relationship with texts. Share a copy of your textual lineage and tell why these texts are important. Have students construct their textual lineages throughout the year. Reflect on the lineage at regular intervals that seem to make the most sense in your instructional environment.

3. Create textual-lineage "starter kits" at all grade levels; that is, identify several texts that pay attention to clearly defined platforms (e.g., defining self, becoming resilient) that honor students' multiple identities. Here are some things to consider as you put them together:
    - The textual lineage starter kits should include texts that will potentially have a sustaining quality for students as they shape their lives.
    - The kits should serve as a frame of reference for African American adolescent males as they learn to move toward individual success and the success of their posterity.
    - The kits should help them engage in a redefining of who they are and what they can become individually and collectively. The ultimate aim of the kit is to move them toward self-determination, collective responsibility, and self-fulfillment as they stretch their humanity and contribute to the welfare of the larger society.

As you will read later, I offered *The Envy of the World* (Cose 2002) as one of the readings in my son's textual lineage starter kit. Cose wrote,

> Being a black man has never been easy. It certainly wasn't easy for our forefathers. Yet at a time when the entire might of a race-demented society conspired to destroy their dignity, millions managed to hold their heads high. They refused to allow their humanity to be stripped away. Every generation has its demons. . . . Many of our demons reside deep within us, invisible yet powerful, eating away at our confidence and sense of self-worth. (5)

I want my son to make the linkage between an historical context and future projections as he wrestles with the role he wants to play. The quote turns the lens inward for an answer, with the intent of having him accept culpability for his future.

Poetic Broadsides

It is impossible to create a formula for the future which does not take into account that our society has been doing something special against the Negro for hundreds of years. How then can he be absorbed into the mainstream of American life if we do not do something for him now, in order to balance the equation and equip him to compete on a just and equal basis?

—MARTIN LUTHER KING, JR.

And I know I am solid and sound,
To me the converging objects of the universe perpetually flow,
All are written to me, and I must get what the writing means.

—WALT WHITMAN

■ **Essential question for students and educators:** How do I connect with my soul so that others and I benefit?

In *Changing Minds*, Howard Gardner (2006) writes, "a key to changing a mind is to produce a shift in the individual's mental representations—the particular way in which a person perceives, codes, retains, and accesses information" (5). Poetry is fast-moving text that can engage African American adolescent males and shift their mental representations of who they are and what they can become. Reading and writing poetry helps these young males find and activate their voices. Poetry also triggers a new understanding about a wide range of topics from the political to the personal to the cultural. Sadly, very few young African American males can name a poem that informs them. Poetry is not part of their textual lineage. The power of poetry remains untapped in many classrooms.

I have carried the following poem, on typewriter paper now yellowed, in my wallet since 1991:

Black Man in America
by Julius Caesar Russell

Again I face the wall
A sight all too familiar in our lives
Sight which I no longer have
Still my vision is correct . . . I focus

The blood of yesterday has blinded me
My eyes have dried shut
Your grip upon my blindfold has tightened
As more nails are added to the scarf
My screams have yet to be answered

No man deserves this, my reasoning for enduring such torture
Another question I cannot answer
I have never pledged my faith to the God Forsaken country

My own brothers cannot see me
I know that they listen, they search, I will be found
Yes, I do have some last words

An opportunity to salvage this moment of silence

U do not deserve my children
You are unworthy of my wife
My existence in this hell on earth
Is an injustice to my manhood and my God

Yet and still
I will not quit, concede, or
I will not let you win
I will not let you win
I am a black man in America

The Shots Ring

A student gave me this poem when I was a college undergraduate. I was walking on the campus of Northern Illinois University when he approached me and said, "I want you to have this." I met the author of the poem (who was also the person who gave it to me) several days later. When I asked him why he had given me the poem, he said, "Because you need it." He had identified me as a young student leader, a self-described warrior fighting for the rights of African American students in my campus leadership roles.

Poetry has sustained me over the years. I used it as an eighth grade teacher, and I continue to use it in professional development presentations. I use poetry with young African American males to help them examine what it means to be human in today's context. During last summer's literacy institute, I had the young males wrestle with descriptors of African American males in order to put together myth-busting broadsides that moved them to define themselves. I also write poems.

Poems that are part of my textual lineage include Claude McKay's "If We Must Die" and "America"; Langston Hughes' "Mother to Son"; Amiri Baraka's "SOS"; and Paul Laurence Dunbar's "We Wear the Mask." Several of these poems have been referred to as "poetic broadsides" (Reid 2002).

In Search of Poetic Broadsides

Teachers often find it difficult to activate African American adolescent males' voices and move them beyond intellectual sterility or intellectual reticence. A teacher's *what's the matter?* is often met by a *nothing* from these young males—an insurmountable impasse beneath which both teacher and student seethe over the inability to build positive relationships in the classroom. Poetic broadsides—short and to the point—can break the impasse. "Broadsides should be prepared for quick reading and should be fitted easily into the back pocket, in case the reader has to stop and be revolutionary" (Reid 2002).

Poetic broadsides have a number of characteristics.

1. They acknowledge pain/poverty fatigue.

2. They are anchored by purpose.

3. They are written out of necessity.

4. They call for the next self-appointed leader—someone to build capacity among us.

5. They ignite protest against self or others.

6. They reject patience and waiting.

Historically, poetic broadsides have spoken out against

- lynching

- violation of black women

- oppressive conditions of humankind

- injustices

- church bombings

- murders of civil rights activists

- police brutality

- moral lapses that erupt as a result of social frustrations

- infiltration of dope into black communities

Historical broadsides, both conventional and nonconventional, were an attempt to fill a number of voids, such as

1. limited knowledge of oneself

2. limited knowledge of oneself in relationship to the rest of the world

3. limited knowledge of powers beyond one's control

4. limited knowledge about how to change one's destiny and the destiny of a people

Filling these massive voids today requires something deeper than what is often offered in classrooms. Poetry can be extremely—uncomfortably—political. Poetry can also be antideath, antiresignation, and anti-acquiescence.

I have challenged African American adolescent males to write poetry

- to stop one bullet,

- to stop one pregnancy,

- to stop one dropout,

- to bring one father home,

- to save one younger brother,

- to . . . (have them fill in the rest).

Poetry, on its way to becoming part of students' textual lineage, can be a clarion call. My poem below is a call for language to define oneself that counters other common descriptors of African American boys in literary and nonliterary texts.

Descriptors

They call me beast.
They call me monster.
I just want to be human.
Give me the language to make my case
Before I cuss you out,
Making you call me an *inarticulate foul-mouth fool,*
Doomed and damned by another descriptor.

In the early morning hours of August 11, 2008, I read the following article in the *Chicago Tribune*:

Maywood Families Mourn 3 Teens Killed in Shooting
Police Seek Clues; Boys Not Known to Be in Gangs

Kent Flowers Jr., 18, was the kind of son who sacrificed going out with friends to help his father build a closet.

When those friends stopped by late Friday night, Flowers went outside his home in the 1900 block of Harrison Street in Maywood and got into a car with them to visit. The night exploded with gunfire and he and two other 18-year-olds, Devin Stokes and Oscar Pritchett, suffered multiple wounds. All three later died at Loyola University Medical Center. The driver was critically injured.

The four were close, each striving for achievement, relatives said. Stokes was to attend Northeastern Illinois University on scholarship this fall, his mother, Theresa Stokes, said Sunday.

Pritchett and the injured driver, whom the Tribune is not naming because he is a witness, were working at O'Hare International Airport, and her son was going to try for a job there too, Stokes said.

"Everything was always about them being together," she said.

The injured man remained at Loyola Sunday, family members said.

He and Devin Stokes had formed the Young Money Club to encourage their peers to succeed honestly, Theresa Stokes said.

"Making money, but doing it legitimately, and not seeking out the gangs, and keeping away from violence," were its goals, she said.

As those close to the young men struggled with their grief, police said they had no information on a motive for the killings. The gunfire came about 12:15 a.m. Saturday. All that marked the spot Sunday were a few shards of glass and a small memorial of flowers, a poster and candles on a ragged elm outside the Flowers' home.

Residents worry these killings and other recent homicides, including one Aug. 4, are reversing a hard-fought decline in crime after several years of increases.

All but Flowers had graduated in the spring from Proviso East High School in Maywood.

Principal Milton Patch said the young men had avoided gangs and were aiming at college or working. Staff members will be "devastated" this week when they return to prepare for the start of the school year next week, he said.

"Things had been getting better, but we're in some sort of mad rash of shootings," Patch said.

Flowers, a visual artist who also rapped, loved schoolwork even though he had some difficulty in completing high school, his parents said.

"He came home, he did his homework—I didn't have to be behind him, because he loved doing his homework," his father, Kent Flowers Sr., said. "I mean, you couldn't ask for more than that. It was not a lot of hard work to get him to do what he had to do."

Upon learning his girlfriend was having a baby, he recommitted himself to school, working toward graduating this coming semester, his family said. Flowers wanted to become a psychologist, his father said.

"Things were changing. He was becoming a man," said his cousin Shunna Hale. "He knew what he needed to do to provide for his family."

Stokes was a chess champion who also was active in the high school drama club, Patch said. The eldest of three children, Stokes recently had been told he was in line for a promotion at the McDonald's in Lombard where he worked, his mother said.

Those who knew the four young men said they cannot point to any reason that they might be targeted. Police said they had no information on whether they had gang ties.

But Patch said they all had pursued their studies vigorously and appeared to have no gang ties. Pritchett, for example, had one detention all last school year, Patch said. Pritchett's family declined to comment.

Flowers had been pressured by schoolmates, his father said, and struggled to figure out how to respond.

Flowers Sr. said the neighborhood has seen violence before, largely because of drug-dealing spurred by people who view the nearby Eisenhower Expressway as an easy escape route.

continues

Both the Flowers and Stokes families said they pray to be able to forgive those who took the lives of their sons. As she spoke to visitors Sunday, Devin Stokes' mother kept her hand on his Bible, which she had found open to a reading from Colossians, including this passage:

"Bear with each other and forgive one another if any of you has a grievance against someone. Forgive as the Lord forgave you."

Family members want to see changes in their village, even though it can't undo the shooting.

"Somebody knows who the perpetrator is. But nobody's saying nothing," Flowers Sr. said. "And everybody's going to keep their mouth shut. The same people keep doing the same thing over and over and over. Something has to be done."

I had heard about the shootings on the news the evening before and had spent a sleepless night. After reading the article, the poem below erupted from my soul.

Checkmate
by Alfred W. Tatum

He taught me how to play chess when I was younger
To make all the right moves
The rooks, the knights, the pawns, the bishops
I could castle and use my ~~bitch~~ my Queen to protect myself
All of these thoughts flashed in my mind when the car pulled up beside us
It's 12:15 a.m.
I am eighteen, sitting on the passenger's side
No where to move, no strategy
I thought about learning chess when I was younger
The young man in the other car lifts his hands—checker hands,
    TIC-TAC-TOE hands
I was no match for him
I thought my scholarship letter would save me—it was my next move
My buddies scream first
I'm hit next
Checkmate—game ov . . .

Using Poetic Broadsides to Activate the Writer's Minds

I shared the words of brother poets from the past with twelve African American adolescent males who participated in last summer's institute hosted by the University of Illinois at Chicago Reading Clinic, poems that I hoped would inspire their writing of poetry and remain with them for a long time. I chose these poetic broadsides as a starting point for building textual lineages because they are short and to the point, the issues they deal with suggested that our time in the institute was going to be serious and thoughtful, and they immediately connected with the students.

Black Art (1966)
by Amiri Baraka

. . .

We want "poems that kill."
Assassin poems,
Poems that shoot guns
Poems that wrestle cops into alleys
And take their weapons leaving them dead
With tongues pulled out and sent to Ireland,
knockoff poems
For dope selling wops or slick halfwhite politicians

◆ ◆ ◆

Untitled (1967)
by Don L. Lee (now Haki Madhubuti)

America calling.
negroes.
can you dance?
play foot/baseball?
nanny?
cook?

continues

needed now. negroes
who can entertain
ONLY.
others not wanted.
(& are considered extremely dangerous.)

◆ ◆ ◆

If We Must Die (1919)
by Claude McKay

If we must die, let it not be like hogs
Hunted and penned in an inglorious spot,
While round us bark the mad and hungry dogs,
Making their mock at our accursed lot.
If we must die, O let us nobly die,
So that our precious blood may not be shed
In vain; then even the monsters we defy
Shall be constrained to honor us though dead!
O kinsmen we must meet the common foe!
Though far outnumbered let us show us brave,
And for their thousand blows deal one deathblow!
What though before us lies the open grave?
Like men we'll face the murderous, cowardly pack,
Pressed to the wall, dying, but fighting back!

◆ ◆ ◆

Questions
by Alfred W. Tatum

Why do you keep asking me so many questions?
Who gives you the right?
Your strange ways are irritating.

Let me ask you a question.
WHY DO YOU KEEP ASKING ME QUESTIONS?
No more questions.
Answers only.
Now, do you still want to talk?

I challenged these young men to read these poems from the perspective of a writer, not a reader. I asked them to use the following questions to guide their thinking about the poems:

1. Is there something about the writing that lingers in the mind?

2. Does the poem have energy?

3. Has the writer taken care to put just the right word or phrase in just the right spot?

4. Does the title match the poem?

5. Can you identify the platform(s) or social justice issue(s) being addressed?

After reading and thinking about the poems, the young men wrote their own poetic broadsides, raising questions about death, genocide, self-hatred, identity development, social responsibility, spirituality, and personal resilience. All but one of the poems below were written during the second day of a five-week institute.

I Am
by Brother Poet I

I speak therefore I think,
I think therefore I am,
Being of existence, I am a voice,
A voice in this world that should be heard,
Outspoken yet underspoken,
I have much to say, but nothing to say at all.

◆ ◆ ◆

Is This What We Have Become
by Brother Poet II

After all the fight and struggle for freedom
Is this what we become
Killing and fighting one another like animals
We should take charge and do something with our lives
If not, what's the point of being free it can do no good for me

bang bang
by Brother Poet III

you hear guns go off
more bodies drop
but
the clock still
goes
tick tock

◆ ◆ ◆

I Hate You
by Brother Poet IV

I hate you
I hate you
I don't like you
You make me sick
You make me feel like I'm getting hit
With a stick
In the head,
Getting sprayed with mace in the face
You make me feel like I'm getting snatched from god's holy grace
That's why I hate

◆ ◆ ◆

Untitled
by Brother Poet V

"Look into my eyes"
With age comes wisdom . . .
So look into my eyes . . .
With every wrinkle in my face, another story lies . . .
I look at you . . . and I see myself . . .
But in an immature state of mind
So eager to enter the world
But, not knowing what the world hides . . .

Beauty isn't just skin deep
It is developed in the mind
Not knowing how truly beautiful you are until you see the ugly inside . . .
I'm confident in myself
And to you I ask why??
Why??
Why kill off your own race?
It's just a form of genocide
My brother I beg you look into my eyes
With every wrinkle in my face another story lies
DAMN IT!!!!!
YOUNG BRUTHA LOOK INTO MY EYES!!!

◆ ◆ ◆

Who's the Man?
by Brother Poet VI

Look at me
Do you respect me?
Am I powerful with this barrel down your throat?
Or are you just intimidated?
I think I'm a man.
At least this is what I see.
They never showed me differently.
Shoot him down so I can get my soccer ball
Or he'll think I'm cool and let me in the gang
Maybe that bully won't bother me.
So please show me what is a man!
Before I pull the trigger again.
BANG!

Poetry and Humanity

In 2001, I worked as a reading specialist in an elementary school on Chicago's West Side. I always attempted to use texts in powerful ways to model instructional practices with teachers. I wanted them to be transformed by text—have a mind-altering, affective experience—during our professional development sessions, because it is difficult to model the power of text if your listeners don't experience that power. I selected Margaret Walker's poem "Lineage" to model using a semantic map.

However, I began by relating a personal anecdote about my favorite uncle. Then I read the poem aloud.

Lineage

My grandmothers were strong.
They followed plows and bent to toil.
They moved through fields sowing seed.
They touched earth and grain grew.
They were full of sturdiness and singing.
My grandmothers were strong.
My grandmothers are full of memories
Smelling of soap and onions and wet clay
With veins rolling roughly over quick hands
They have many clean words to say.
My grandmothers were strong.
Why am I not as they?

After they had listened to the poem, I asked these teachers to close their eyes and think about a favorite relative and a favorite memory they had of this person. Then I asked them to write about this relative the way Margaret Walker wrote about her grandmothers.

The first volunteer to share her story was a woman of German descent. She began to talk about her grandfather who was murdered during the Holocaust. Several lines into her reading, she began to cry uncontrollably. Her colleagues comforted her, as I stood near the front of the room in tears.

The semantic map was abandoned; there was no need for it. The power was in the poem, twelve lines written by Margaret Walker, that led us to embrace one another. We became human together not because of some standard-based need to interpret poetry, but because we recognized the need to connect in the moment we shared together. I am indebted to Margaret Walker for that moment—her poem was worth reading.

It is my hope that we share poetry worth reading with African American adolescent males, poems that will become part of their textual lineage, poems that will move us closer to them as they get to know themselves—even the ones who are having difficulty in life. A young brother poet who participated in a summer institute reminds us of the need to pay urgent attention to the immediate.

Life Is
by Brother Poet II

Little
Inconveniences
Full-blown
Emergencies
Life is hard
Love
Inspiring
Fate
Everlasting feelings
Life is wonderful
Living it for the now
In the spirit of the moment
Fun
Exciting
Life is breathtaking

To me there is no real definition for life but whatever it is, it's worth living. Are poems now a vital part of his textual lineage? Only time will tell. But he's off to a good start.

Productive Starting Points

1. Reconnect African American adolescent males to their rich poetic tradition. Find ways to incorporate poetry into discussions of literary and nonliterary texts.

2. Read poems to students to nurture an appreciation for the genre.

3. Encourage African American males to use poetry as a tool for communicating—that is, to find ways to use language in beautiful and melodic ways.

4. Encourage students to write poetic broadsides they can revisit when times and events dictate.

Short Stories

■ **Essential question for students and educators:** What is the role of individuals in igniting a social movement?

Are we confined by our times?

Are we confined by our context?

We had never had instruction in literary matters at school; the literature of the nation or the Negro had never been mentioned. My schoolmates could not understand why anyone would want to write a story; and, above all, they could not understand why I had called it *The Voodoo of Hell's Half-Acre*. The mood out of which a story was written was the most alien thing conceivable to them. They looked at me with new eyes, and a distance, a suspiciousness came between us. If I had thought anything in writing the story, I had thought perhaps it would make me more acceptable to them, and now it was cutting me off from them more completely than ever.

—RICHARD WRIGHT

While doing research for this book, I discovered a short story by Walter Myers in the edited anthology *What We Must See* (Coombs 1971). He was not the beloved young-adult novelist Walter *Dean* Myers then; he and the writers of the other stories were relatively unknown and unpublished. In his introduction, Coombs wrote:

These short stories speak of [the] urban slums and the rural farms. They speak of the abuse of a people who know hopelessness and fear and love. They speak of the harrowing search for identity, of growing strong, of being determined to live, and of fighting, ultimately for one's life. (xi)

I was struck by the care the young Myers took with his writing and by the words he chose to convey the humanity of three characters in just fourteen pages. His biography at the back of the edited volume read, "like all Black artists, trying to survive artistically and [physically] in an environment which seems as hostile to art as it is to Blackness" (208).

The short story was the river by which many African American writers traveled, the fire that lit their way—it was the true standard of the Harlem Renaissance (Gable 2004). African American writers of short fiction who have been widely anthologized include W. E. B. Du Bois, Jean Toomer, Zora Neale Hurston, Chester Himes, Langston Hughes, Richard Wright, and Sonia Sanchez. These authors and many others have used the short story to discuss ideas, morals, and perspectives; find and explore identities; change men's minds; speak truth; contemplate both the personal and communal self; and make sense of the times in which they lived and the times yet to be (Gable 2004; King 1972; Naylor 1995). Much of their work, if not all, has been lost on African American adolescent males.

Resurrecting the Short Story

What happened to the short story? In all the textual lineages I have asked African American adolescent males to construct over the years, the short story has been noticeably absent. The tradition of reading and writing short stories has been extinguished. African American adolescent males are not reading or writing short stories that they find meaningful and significant. This is unfortunate, because there are several advantages of using short stories to build students' textual lineages.

1. They are short.

2. They often deal with a single event.

3. They can be managed and paced more effectively in classrooms that include struggling, marginalized, and reluctant readers.

4. They are great tools for modeling writing.

5. They are a great means by which to wrestle with issues of social justice.

6. They provide more experiences with a wide range of texts.

7. They are authentic opportunities for teachers to write and share their writing with students.

Below are two *black shorts* (a term the students and I coined) that I wrote and used as examples during an African American adolescent male summer literacy institute at the University of Illinois at Chicago Reading Clinic. Both stories are written from the perspective of a teenage boy.

Sixteen

by Alfred W. Tatum

She sat two rows in front of me on the seven-car train moving toward the city. Her hair was uncombed, and there were naps all along her two-toned neck. Her daughter's hair was not in much better shape; she probably just didn't have time to get to it this morning. She had earplugs in her ears, and small gold hoop earrings, nothing extravagant, hung from her lobes. The dimples on her moderately dark face were attractive. She was really pretty. She looked like she was about sixteen. I made eye contact with her, and we exchanged a brief smile that was interrupted when the young boy on her lap began to scream; the pacifier had dropped from his mouth. It was obvious he hadn't yet had his first haircut, and the white, dry snot marks on his nose looked nasty. She spent the rest of the ride trying to calm him down. The other passengers, mostly white, looked irritated because the young boy's cries were intruding on their attempts to read the newspaper, work on their laptops, or enjoy their four-dollar cups of coffee. I felt sort of sad for the girl as she bounced the baby up and down on her lap while her little girl looked on. The mother's face tightened each time the shrieks grew louder, and her eyes darted around apologetically. At one point, even I became irritated. *Why won't the boy just shut up?*

"What's your son's name?" I asked as I helped her carry a large bag off the train.

"Emanuel, but we call him Man-Man for short."

"That's his daddy's name, but my daddy's name is Bootsey," the little girl said.

"Shut up, Tee-Tee. I told you about talking so much."

"Are you meeting his father down here?"

"Naw, we don't talk anymore."

"My grandma is picking us up."

"Didn't you hear me tell you to shut up?"

I helped her carry the bag through the crowded terminal as people rushed by us on both sides. We looked like a young couple with two kids. I wanted to carry the bag out to the street and wait with her, but I had to catch the number 60 bus that ran every thirty minutes. I would be late if I chatted any longer. I patted Man-Man on the head and said, "Take care, little fella."

"Bye."

"Bye, Tee-Tee."

"Thank you for helping me with the bag."

"No problem."

"What's your name?"

"Richard," I said before turning and walking in the other direction. As I reached the revolving doors, I heard the boy begin to cry again, and thought about my own situation.

I was sure I was about to do the right thing.

It was hard to imagine what my girlfriend wanted to do; I didn't understand her logic. We had been together since our freshman year. There was no way I was going to be like my old man or her old man. I got her pregnant on purpose just to prove my point. She knew it too, but I convinced her that everything would be okay. We argued a lot because she kept letting her mother and girlfriends get into our business.

"How we gonna take care a baby?"

"You'll see, everything is gonna be okay as soon as we finish school."

"Where you gonna work with a high school diploma?"

"I'll get a job. Don't worry about that."

"What about college?"

"We don't need college to take care of no baby."

"Where we gonna live?"

"It'll work out, trust me."

I replayed this conversation in my mind over and over as I waited at the bus stop. *Where's the bus? I got to hurry up and get to the clinic; I can't let her do it.* It was all running through my head—Man-Man's crying, Tee-Tee's talking, my girlfriend's questions. I reached into my pockets for the fare card my momma had to give me so I could make this trip today, and a new thought started messing with me. *I had no money. Still, I wasn't going to be like my old man, or Man-Man's daddy, or Bootsey. I got myself into this, and I will handle my business.* "Where is the bus?" I muttered impatiently, out loud this time. I had to stop her.

I looked at the other people gathered at the bus stop. Were they carrying burdens like me? It was difficult to tell. Stepping into the street, I could see the number 60 finally rolling my way. At last. The doors opened and several passengers got off. A baby on the bus was crying, a baby being held by someone who looked like me. "Are you getting on, young man?" the driver asked. "No, I'm waitin' on the number 120." The bus rolled away, and I walked back toward the train station.

Flow of Traffic
by Alfred W. Tatum

I could always see the steady stream of traffic below my window. But I never asked where the traffic was going until yesterday after the notice came. It was the same notice my friend, Butchy, received. Then he was gone. It was always rumored that these bricks would come tumbling down. The stories behind the bricks will always be there, but the old brown bricks will soon be replaced with the new, more expensive bricks. The closets behind the new bricks will be larger, and the faces behind the bricks will look much different.

I asked my mother, "Mom, are we coming back after the new bricks are up?" She just said, "I don't want to live here anymore. It won't be the same." Deep down I know that she would have trouble affording the new bricks on her salary. There is a beautiful sign down the block that reads, "New Homes Starting at $475,000." I like the pictures on the sign, but that's a lot of money. I guess it costs a lot of money to replace a boy's memories.

I remember when me and Butchy first met. We were four. I moved in on the sixth floor the same day he moved in on the fifth. He rushed into the elevator when the doors were about to close. "Come on, Momma. The doors are about to close." His mother, Miss Brown, yelled, "You almost got slammed in those doors, boy. I told you to stop that running." He looked sad for a moment, until he remembered he had a red popsicle in his hand. He looked over at me when he heard me ask, "Mom, can I have a popsicle like him?" I could still hear the music coming from the ice cream truck outside. "Not right now, boy," she said. Butchy said I could have some of his. I said, "I can't eat off yo' popsicle." That's when he pulled another one out of his back pocket. It was one of those popsicles that come two in a package. My mom told me it was okay. That's when my mom met Miss Brown. They both looked so young and happy like they could be anything in the world. Butchy and I have been together every day it seems since we met on the elevator ten years ago. He moved out two months ago and I haven't heard from him since.

He didn't move out in a moving truck. There were two vans and a car packed with stuff. He squeezed in the back seat of the car with his face near the window on the passenger side. I felt scared. He didn't leave a telephone number so I could stay in touch. We never needed a phone number before. I could always walk down to the fifth floor or see him at school. We came outside every day at almost the same time to shoot some hoops. I am better than him because of my jumper. I am also a few inches taller, but he's a little quicker than me.

I remember we used to talk about going to the league. I was going to be a forward and he was going to run point. We had to go to the right college, though. You couldn't jump to the league from high school anymore. We thought that was a bunch of crap. You can be a pro tennis player without college, but not go to the league. We thought it was because more black men were skipping college and going to the league. The brothers probably wanted to be able to afford some of the new bricks for them and their mommas. We figured that we would both go to the University of North Carolina or Duke. They are always the powerhouses. I also liked the thought of going to California, maybe UCLA.

California girls look so pretty to me. It's like they are always dressed in shorts and have on bright colors. I am going to have a bright red sports car with a drop-top and booming sound. You have to have a fine girl, a dime piece, with a car like that. My mom heard me sharing my dream with Butchy one day and she yelled out, "And it better not be a white girl." I yelled back, "It's *definitely* going to be a white girl or maybe Asian." I like to tease my mom. I had never really thought about white girls or Asian girls, I just thought about a beautiful girl with a cute smile, pretty nails, nice legs, and long hair. Mom, always needing the last word, yelled again, "She better be a sista like your momma so your babies can be as fine as me." Strange for her to say that because I never even thought about babies—just the league, a red car, and a fine lady.

When we got older Butchy stopped talking about the league all the time like he used to. His game starting falling off when he started getting involved with other stuff. We were still tight, but we didn't hang out as much on the court. I don't think he could wait another four more years to start getting paid. He wanted the money now. It was easy to make a little money in front of the old bricks.

Living in the old bricks became rougher and rougher as we got older. I started hating living here sometimes, but it was home. This is where I learned to ride my bike. This is where I earned my first trophy. Where I got my first kiss, from Tammie. I can still smell the bubble gum she had in her mouth. I went in to press my lips against her lips and she stuck her tongue in my mouth. It was a strange sensation, but it felt nice. From then on, I knew I was a French kisser. I hated when Tammie moved out. Her family left six months ago for one of the suburbs. She didn't leave a number for me either. She would have been a nice girl to ride around with in California.

We are one of the last families in the Wells. Wells is short for the Ida B. Wells Housing Project, on the South Side of Chicago. There is no more barbeque smoke in the Wells. No more block parties. Two of the elementary schools closed because they had too few kids. Momma was holding out on moving because she don't think it's right to have to be forced out of a place. She wants to leave on her own terms. She also wants me to graduate from eighth grade first. I know she has a lot of memories in the Wells too.

But I really think she's scared. She's lived here all her life. There's something familiar about the bricks that's becoming less familiar, but something is still familiar. We are close to the bus line that takes Momma downtown where she works. We can walk to the lakefront in the summer. There are more and more white people walking and riding their bikes along the lakefront. I remember it being all black people on the lakefront. I thought it was good to see different people. I didn't see it as a sign of things to come. The older folks in the neighborhood would talk about a conspiracy going on to take the lakefront back. I just saw it as God's lakefront that belonged to anybody who wanted to take advantage of it. I was not into all that race talk. But it is true that there are fewer and fewer black people on the lakefront. Maybe there's something to this conspiracy. I think it's a conspiracy against poor people, not black people. I don't see poor and black as being the same thing. I see poor as being poor and black as being black. The two sometimes collide, but they are not synonymous as some people think.

Barack Obama is black, but he's not poor. Kobe is black. The owner of the Charlotte Bobcats is black. Some people say, "But that's different."

When they say that, I start to think that maybe some people have a conspiracy against themselves. I know Momma likes the pictures of the new bricks even though she talks bad about them. They are just too expensive for her. Being squeezed out makes her mad. Her two jobs just don't pay enough.

I know money is a problem because she always tells me that I don't have any brothers or sisters because it's too expensive to raise kids these days. She even complains when I eat up the food too fast. I can't help it. I am growing, and I hate to be hungry. It just does not seem right to be hungry in a world where people are buying two-bedroom homes starting at $475,000. Sometimes I wish I could walk up to someone and say, "I'll take two of those, please." I need one for me and Mom, the other one for Butchy and Miss Brown. We can all live right next door to each other.

Mom doesn't smile as much as she used too. Laughter once filled our apartment. I think she's lonely. She might be overworked. Maybe she's overworked *and* lonely. She does not have a boyfriend because she does not want any man who is not my daddy raising me. I tell her having a boyfriend would be cool. She says she does not have time for a man while she is working two jobs. But I am thinking if a real man was around she wouldn't have to work two jobs. The problem is she can't find that good man around the old bricks. The men around here are struggling too and trying to figure out how Momma can help them instead of finding a way to help Momma.

I bet she would like to have a date at that new Starbucks on 35th Street where they sell four-dollar cups of coffee. It would be nice for someone to buy Mom one of those cups and a bagel. I would love to see her sitting in front of the large glass window, laughing and smiling. This might make her feel like the neighborhood is changing with her, not against her. She can listen to the conversations of the white patrons who are not talking about some conspiracy against black people, but chatting about the same things all people talk about. I am sure they are talking about family, gas prices, Obama and McCain's presidential race, and other stuff all people talk about when they get together over a cup of coffee. I am going to try to make enough money to take Mom to Starbucks. I think she would like that.

"Son, where did you put the notice?" Mom is on her cell phone talking to a friend from her job who's going to help us move. She can't remember if we have to be out on July 7 or July 17. I can't find the notice, but I tell her we have to be out by July 7. I remember because it is three days after the fourth of July. No more fireworks on the playground. I start to laugh because I remember when Butchy held a firecracker too long in his hand. I told him to throw it, but he pushed it to the limit. He still has a mark on his index finger. I wonder where they shoot fireworks in the place where we are going. Mom is still trying to find a place. She talks about how everything is so expensive. She's never had to pay a gas bill like most of the places she's looked at require. This is a major transition. She sat up one night adding everything up—rent, carfare, food, cell phone, cable, electricity, and gas bill. No money left over for Starbucks or fun. I wish I could get a summer job to help out in the new neighborhood. They say it's easier to get a job in the suburbs. I hope there is a gym where I can play ball indoors or play in a summer tournament. The tournament would have to be free. I don't see myself asking Mom for the money right now.

Well, tomorrow is moving day. Our stuff is packed. This is my last night in the Wells. I am sad, but kind of happy. There was a shooting last night. Eddie is dead. He was good enough to make it to the league when he was younger, but he stopped playing ball when the bricks came tumbling down around him. I almost feel like crying, but I can't. We're moving to a place called Hazel Crest. It's far away from downtown, but Mom thinks it will be safer for me. She also found a place where the gas bill is included in the rent. An older black couple wanted to rent out their two-bedroom house. The house has a backyard with a fence around it. I was excited when we visited because I saw a pretty girl who lived in the house across the street. She would look nice in a red car with me. She is a sista so I know that will make Mom happy.

Two weeks ago, it felt like all the old bricks were tumbling down around us. Mom was getting depressed brick after brick after brick after brick. I stared out the window each night looking at the flow of traffic wondering where it would take us. There's something funny about traffic. It flows in all directions. Sometimes you just have to get in it and see where it takes you. I wonder where it took Butchy and Tammie. I wonder where it will take Mom. I wonder where it will take me. I hope we all meet up one day to talk about it at Starbucks back on 35th Street where the journey began.

After reading "Flow of Traffic," one young male told me, "I would read it if it were in a short story book. It was kind of related to Chicago. Actually, it is depressing. All of his friends are leaving and stuff." I had watched him as he read the story, heard him laugh. He told me he laughed when they all end up on 35th Street, because the language was familiar.

Gentrification and community displacement are real problems in many of the U.S.'s big cities. And the surrounding suburban school districts have the challenge of addressing the literacy needs of African American adolescent males from economically depressed communities who are entering unfamiliar schools and unfamiliar communities. The history of the role of texts in the lives of African American men faced with new challenges is our guide for using short literary and nonliterary texts to build students' textual lineages in order to help them become resilient and find direction.

Canvassing the Historical Landscape

Langston Hughes (1967) edited the classic anthology *The Best Short Stories by Black Writers, 1899–1967*. This was my short story bible as an eighth grade teacher. I have a worn copy littered with annotations and sticky notes.

- *Almos' a Man*, by Richard Wright
  The first movement he made the following morning was to reach under the pillow for the gun. In the gray light of dawn he held it loosely, feeling a sense of power. Could killa man wida gun like this. Kill anybody, black or white. And if he were holding this gun in his hand nobody could run him over; they would have to respect him. (96)

- *Thank You, M'am*, by Langston Hughes
  "But you put yourself in contact with *me*," said the woman. "If you think that that contact is not going to last awhile, you got another thought coming. When I get through with you, sir, you are going to remember Mrs. Luella Bates Washington Jones." (71)

- *The Revolt of the Evil Fairies*, by Ted Poston
  Yet I was inconsolable the first time they turned me down for Prince Charming. That was the year they picked Roger Jackson. Roger was not only dumb; he stuttered. But he was light enough to pass for white, and that was apparently sufficient. (87)

- *The Almost White Boy*, by Willard Motley
  By birth he was Negro and half white. Socially he was all Negro. That is when people knew that his mother was a brownskin woman with

straightened hair and legs that didn't respect the color line when it came to making men turn around to look at her. (134)

- ◆ *The Pocketbook Game*, by Alice Childress
  Day's work is an education! Well, I mean workin' in different homes you learn much more than if you was steady in one place. . . . I tell you, it really keeps your mind sharp tryin' to watch for what folks will put over on you. (205)

- ◆ *Marijuana and a Pistol*, by Chester Himes
  He started giggling and then began to laugh and laugh and laugh until his guts retched because it was such a swell idea, so amazingly simple and logical and perfect that it was excruciatingly funny that he had never thought of it before—he would stick up the main offices of the Cleveland Trust Company at Euclid and Ninth with two beer bottles in his pockets. (104)

In 1927, George Schuyler wrote the masterful short story "Lynching for Profit," in which a character makes a plea for taking advantage of the money-making possibilities for one of the nation's most heinous crimes, lynching. It's a strong model, as the excerpt below from Craig Gable's *Ebony Rising* (2004) shows:

And how can we do this? Well, you all know that the news of a lynching to be held always draws a large audience of white people. They will come from miles around to see that justice is done, and perhaps to carry a souvenir back home. I have known hangings and burnings in this state to have drawn spontaneous gatherings of as high as 2,000 people.

Now if it is possible to bring together that many people to witness a lynching with only by-word-of-mouth advertising, why isn't it possible to bring about 50,000 people from all parts of the state by inaugurating the same advertising methods we have found so potent with soap, underwear, cigarettes, and overalls? Why can't we do it? Why can't we make this practice more profitable? Why can't we inject the spirit of service into it? That's the word, gentlemen—Service! (216)

Reading this short story, I momentarily forgot it was fiction. The author had me where he wanted me—deeply engaged and invested in his words, a place we want all students. I fumed at the gripping advertisement Schuyler created:

NEGRO TO BE BURNED AT STAKE
In Moronville, Ga.
At the Cretin County Fairgrounds
Come One!   Come All!
Bring the Family and Spend a Pleasant Day.
Plenty of Refreshments Served.

———

Excursions from All Neighboring Towns at Half Price.
Street Cars Will Take You Directly to the Fairgrounds.

———

COME AND SEE THE GHASTLY SIGHT!
HEAR THE BLACK VILLAIN SCREAM!

SMELL THE ROASTING FLESH!
TAKE HOME A KNUCKLE OR RIB!

———

ADMISSION ONE DOLLAR
Including War Tax.
A Seat for Every Man, Woman, and Child.
Come and Be Comfortable—No Rowdyism.
Perfect Order Will Be Maintained by
THE MORONVILLE POLICE DEPARTMENT.
(Gable, 2004, 217–218)

The authors of these short stories lived with their eyes and ears open as they wrestled with contemporary issues. Therefore, it makes sense to have African American adolescent males read these classic short stories primarily as writers. The content may be dated, but seeing how the writers constructed the stories is an excellent model for writing about things happening today. The authors of these stories had to wrestle with several questions:

1. What are today's most pressing issues?

2. How do I use language to write a story that feels authentic?

3. How do I situate my story?

4. How do I make the point I am trying to make within a few pages?

Getting African American Adolescent Males to Read and Write Short Stories

During the institutes I conduct for young African American adolescent males, I use examples of short stories to help us study the genre. We read several paragraphs together as writers and discuss how to begin a short story. Then I challenge the young men to write a short story that both

1. stops readers in their tracks with bold, unapologetic writing; and

2. makes readers listen without telling them they have to listen (the words do the work).

Let me walk you through the lesson.

Studying the Genre

First I project a slide of the first paragraph of a short story:

> Lil Joe sat in the back of the car with a stupid look on his face. The way he dressed marked him as a young man looking for trouble. The bulky bag he was toting probably raised suspicion as he trotted down the street close to midnight. He began to think about his mother's reaction to his being in trouble. Although unwarranted, he felt the weight of her disappointment. He was excited and scared at the same time. He now had a story to share with his friends. Many of them often talked about their first time. He was always left out of the conversation. He wondered if his experience as a "first timer" would allow him to become part of the brotherhood.

I tell the students what the paragraph does:

1. A character is named early on.

2. There are details that situate the story.

3. Momentum is established.

4. The following critical elements are included:
   - structure
   - dialogue
   - description

Keeping Readers Involved

Then I show another slide—the first paragraphs of "Liars Don't Qualify," by Junius Edwards—in which the things Edwards does to hook his readers are highlighted.

> Will Harris[1] sat on the bench in the waiting room for another hour. His pride was not the only thing that hurt.[2a] He wanted them to call him in and get him registered so he could get out of there. Twice, he started to go into the inner office and tell them, but he thought better of it.[2b] He had counted ninety-six cigarette butts[2c] on the floor when a fat man come out of the office and spoke to him.
> "What you want, boy?"[3]
> Will Harris got to his feet.
> "I came to register."[3]

1. Will Harris is introduced immediately.

2. Details build momentum and situate the story:
   a. His pride was not the only thing hurt.
   b. Twice, he started to go into the inner office.
   c. Ninety-six cigarette butts

3. There is an example of dialogue.

Writing the First Paragraph

Next I ask them to write the first paragraph of their own story. I give them the following outline to help keep them on course:

1. Think of a contemporary social justice issue.

2. Decide on a platform.
   a. Defining self
   b. Becoming resilient
   c. Engaging others
   d. Building capacity

3. Establish a character.

4. Build momentum early on.

5. Write your first paragraph.

6. Share with a brother author and get feedback.

7. Share your first paragraph with the whole group.

Below are two examples of stories my students have written as a result of this lesson.

The Better Option
by Brother Author I

Bobby Helmis was a smart boy but he made stupid decisions. He was on the corner waiting for his next "customers" when his phone rang. He answered; it was his friend John. "Bobby, I just got—" Click. His friend hung up and while Bobby wondered what happened, he did not pay any thought to a man with bloody shoes and a gun in his hand walking by.

Bobby hated violence but felt like he had no choice. Later on that day he found out John was killed by another group of boys that sold drugs and felt that Bobby and his friends were taking their business. Bobby was infuriated when he found out. In his mind he thought he had two options. Option one was to kill the group and get revenge. Option two, he could try and resolve the war with talk instead of violence. He never thought of option three when he could try and help the community by getting a real job that did not hurt the community, and possibly convince others to do the same.

He thought about it, and fell asleep. When he woke up he was as mad as ever. His brown eyes were filled with hate and rage. He chose option one—grabbed a gun and went out to get his friends to prepare them for war. Bobby and his friends went to the block the killers lived on. Bobby gave a signal and they shot at every house that was on the block not thinking of the innocent. The boys ran out their house when they heard gunshots and were shot on sight. Many were killed; blood splattered everywhere. Once Bobby saw what happened he felt bad and angry with what he had done. Suddenly a group of boys came out their house and shot back at them; as Bobby realized what happened he felt it was his fault.

Within the next five minutes Bobby realized that if he wanted to survive he would need to retreat, so he ran to the side of the gunshots, trying to avoid the dead bodies that lay on the ground. He hid behind a tree and sat there with a gun in his hand. A thought of suicide went through his brain as he sat there wondering if this would be the only way to avoid jail and if he should go through with it or not. All of a sudden all the bullets stopped flying and it was silent. Bobby turned around and saw everyone on the cold hard ground either dead or dying. He heard a click and turned his head to see a man with a gun to his head. The man had a bloody arm with a gun wound. The man pulled the trigger and right before the bullet hit, Bobby woke up with a scream.

After seeing his future with option one, Bobby chose option two, stupidly overlooking option three. He went and tried to settle his feud. He went on the block the boys lived on. He spoke to one boy and suggested that an alliance would be best. The boy pulled out a gun and said, *I like this way best,* and again right before the bullet hit he woke up.

After being shot twice he finally thought of option three. Bobby decided to take charge. He threw out all the drugs he possessed. When he tried to convince his friends to do the same they called him crazy but after viewing other options he was determined to go to college and make something of himself. Six years later he finished community college and became a mentor for juvenile kids and saved his community one child at a time.

Un-Identifiable
by Brother Author II

I'm sweating.

The pressure is extreme, and all eyes are on me. I've never had *this* much attention, and right now I don't want it. I'm the victim, and the people out there are my audience. As they wait and see what the verdict is going to be, I can't help but wait with them. I look out and see angry family members and friends look back at me. I wish they wouldn't look at me like that; it makes me feel guilty, un-human. I'm the beast, and they're the pupils, laughing at my disfigurement, making me feel less than what I am! I wish I could tell them what happened. I just wish I could . . . The lady comes into the room and everyone stands up. After she says something, we all sit down. Some dude starts speaking about a right hand and a court of law. The lady gets into her big, black, comfortable leather seat, and she has some type of tool that looks like a wooden hammer in her hands. She just thinks she's so cool, because she's able to have all of these fancy tools, and because we're supposed to respect her. But I don't, and I don't have to. Because of her, I'm here. So it's all her fault . . .

The lady starts to talk, and I can't help but notice her irritating scratchy voice. I drown her out, because I don't want to hear a word that she says. I look into the crowd, and at my family. *Don't listen to what she says. At the end of the day, we'll be left standing, we'll get through everything that has happened*, I thought. After I snap out of my trance, I notice that all eyes are on me. Yet again. This time, I sweat real hard, and people can notice it. Then, she starts talking again:

"Mr. Washington, in the case of . . . "

I drown her out. No! I can't hear her. I don't want to hear her. I wish I was home. I wish I could fast-forward the moment, or rewind to the part when everything was perfect. Everybody was happy. But then I realize that I cannot do that, so I have to accept it . . .

"You are found . . . "

I close my eyes, here it is. Here is the moment that everyone has been waiting on . . .

They come over and take me out of the stands, and I'm yelling. I'm getting closer to the door, and my fate is almost over . . .

They open the door . . .

I sneak a look at my mom, and just before the door closes, I can tell that she is crying . . .

Guilt.

That was all that I was feeling after I left the room.

It's funny. That when you actually do something, you don't think about it until you have to suffer the consequences. After looking back at what I have done, I have the violent flashbacks appear in my eyes. I wish so bad that I hadn't done what I did, but I guess my emotions got the best of me, and I couldn't do anything to stop it.

I feel sorry for the victim's family, I ruined a life, and on top of that, I ruined my own life.

There is a saying out there that relates to my situation. Every stupid mistake that someone has made, every stupid thing that has been said, just remember this: in life, there is no room for error.

In my life, I made a *big* error, and right now, I have to pay for it . . .

Becoming Connected to Short Stories

The fourteen-year-old and the fifteen-year-old who wrote the stories above were becoming connected to short stories. They were dealing with the platforms of defining self, becoming resilient, and building capacity. Before the institute, neither gave any evidence of having made a connection to short stories. One was a self-prophetic lyricist who enjoyed writing rhymes; the other preferred writing longer, extended pieces after having won several young-author contests. Within a relatively short period they began to connect and allow short stories to bellow from within them, bellowing that has been part of the African American male literacy tradition—a tradition that is now lost and needs to be resurrected.

Productive Starting Points

1. Write—and have students write—short stories that define their times and define their contexts.

2. Model and encourage students to read short stories from a writer's perspective.

Armed for Battle

Writing this book, I found myself bound, hemmed in, and encircled by one essential question: *What texts do I want to send my sons off with as they grow up, head off to college, enter a world of their choosing?* Do I send them off with the same texts that equipped me for the world (see Figure 8.1)? Have times changed or have they remained the same?

My older son is in middle school. He has a wide range of interests, and his experiences growing up are quite different than mine were. Based on his interests, our ongoing conversations about current events, and his growing awareness and acceptance of being a young African American adolescent male (partly from media images and partly his own experiences) I prepared a middle school "textual-lineage-building packet" that included seven texts listed below. The texts were selected to provide him with balanced views about contemporary issues, views that will serve as a frame of reference for our continued conversations. For example, Sharon Flake's *Bang* was chosen to help him understand the effects of some of the gun violence occurring in the Chicago Public Schools. Close to seventy CPS students were killed over the course of two school years. Flake's opening lines are

> They kill people where I live. They shoot 'em dead for no real reason. You don't duck you die. That's what happened to my brother Jason. He was seven. Playing on the front porch. Laughing. Then some man ran by yelling, "He gonna kill me. He's gonna—" (2005, 1)

Her text, using the voice of a young man, has a way of sensitizing him to the pain others may feel as a result of loss attributed to gun violence. I wanted him to recognize that gun violence is not normal, and that it needs to be looked at through a human lens that requires real solutions.

Juan Williams' nonfiction text *Enough* provides a different lens for him to think about. In it, Williams writes,

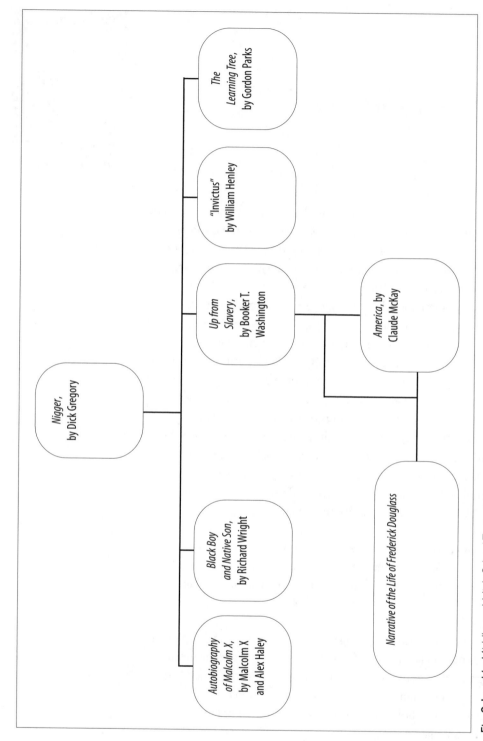

Fig. 8.1: *My Middle and High School Textual Lineage**

*Other texts not displayed are *To Kill a Mockingbird* by Harper Lee, *Of Mice and Men* by John Steinbeck, *Mythology* by Edith Hamilton, and *The Adventures of Huckleberry Finn* by Mark Twain. Each had a profound effect on me.

Real people—children are being hurt. Even if they can't read, those children are smart enough to know they are being treated like deadwood warehoused in bad schools where they are told they'll be promoted to the next grade as long as they don't do drugs, fight, or bring guns to school. Any rational person, even the most trusting child, has to feel alienated from a system that is so heartless. (2006, 103)

I selected these texts because they have the potential to provide my son with emotional and intellectual armament that can be viewed as legitimate because of the messages he encounters in his daily life. He will learn from *Enough* that

1. Black people make up thirteen percent of the population.

2. A black male child born in 2001 has a thirty-three percent chance of going to prison.

3. Seventy percent of black mothers are single parents.

This is why I selected both literary and nonliterary texts. Whereas Frederick Douglass' narrative provides an historical example of becoming resilient (one of the platforms I use when identifying texts for African American adolescent males), Angela Johnson's *The First Part Last* (2003) provides a contemporary example. The key is for me to effectively mediate the text so that the threads begin to bind. I purposely selected texts that were developmentally appropriate and cognitively challenging, texts selected to help him respond to the questions "What does all of this mean?" and "What does all of this mean for me?" He will ultimately be the judge, as I was with my own textual lineage.

1. *Bang* by Sharon Flake

2. *Enough* by Juan Williams

3. *Handbook for Boys* by Walter Dean Myers

4. *Letters to a Young Brother* by Hill Harper

5. *Narrative of the Life of Frederick Douglass* by Frederick Douglass

6. *The Envy of the World* by Ellis Cose

7. *The First Part Last* by Angela Johnson

But what about other young males? What seven texts would I offer to the young man who says, "Fuck academics," or the one who says, "We don't have education on our side." Both may need to build their academic and personal resilience. Should they be reading the same texts or something different? Do I have the right list to give to teachers who ask, "Is there a list you would recommend?" Where is the list?

- Where is the list of texts that will counteract hundreds of years of the miseducation of the Negro in the United States?

- Where is the list that will wipe away the residual effects of race-based slavery?

- Where is the list that will counteract poverty and years of poor schooling?

- Where is the list that will save the souls of many African American adolescent males who are in conflict with themselves, their communities, and the larger society as they travel step-by-step through life and all it has to offer?

- Where is the list that will join educators and African American adolescent males in a communal literacy collaborative in both segregated and integrated settings across racial and gender lines?

Being in the World Without

I also wrestled with other dilemmas. What if I put my imprimatur on texts that miss the mark? There are real lives at stake. So I stepped back to reflect again on my lineage and the scores of lineages I have collected; I imagined what life would be like without the influence of certain texts.

There are several authors I cannot imagine being in the world without. I have come to rely on them for sustenance and strength during my adult life. Du Bois and Baldwin are at the top of that list because they help frame my thinking about the challenges for strengthening the identities of African American males and the triumphs when such identities are strengthened. They are authors I can run to for understanding and guidance. Others have played lesser roles (I am still endeared to Judy Blume's *Are You There God? It's Me Margaret* [1970]). And in recent years, as I continue to struggle to find my place in the world, make a contribution to humanity, and exercise my right *just to be,* I have come to trust several other authors. Toni Morrison and J. M. Coetzee are two such newfound brother and sister authors. I find comfort in their words as they make me feel uneasy, cynical, unknowing, and hopeful—all at the same time. Morrison is teaching me about African American women. I sympathize and empathize with Sula and Seth, female protagonists in her novels *Sula* (2004) and *Beloved* (1987).

I thought I went into the world fairly well equipped. However, as my journey continues, I wonder if I too have suffered from an underexposure to texts. Are there more brother and sister authors I have yet to meet? Who made the decision to share certain texts and neglect others? Did schools do all they could for me? (I'm not sure, but I am convinced that they did enough.) Were my teachers limited by the thinking of the 1970s and 1980s? Are we suffering from the same limitations?

Where would the United States be without the writings of Thomas Jefferson and Thomas Paine and the ideal of religious freedom? Many of our nation's principles and ideals have been codified in documents that sustain the American people and the democratic ideal, an ideal worth fighting and dying for. But there are also less savory texts, such as Article 1, Section 2, Clause 3 of the U.S. Constitution, in which African Americans are considered less than whole citizens:

> Representatives and direct taxes shall be appointed among several States which may be included within this Union, according to their respective Numbers, which shall be determined by adding to the whole Number of free Persons, including those bound to Service for a term of years, and excluding Indians not taxed, *three fifths of all other Persons.* [my emphasis]

Our ever growing nation has been and continues to be peppered with texts. Maya Angelou's poem at Bill Clinton's inauguration is a festoon of America's beautiful constituencies. A single word, *nigger* (veiled by the expression *the N word*), continues to makes this nation uneasy. English teachers continue to do battle to preserve the texts of William Shakespeare and create barriers against other texts. As the nation becomes more racialized/deracialized (depending on the lens one looks through), selecting the right texts for our young people becomes increasingly more complex. Can we ever achieve culturally responsive pedagogy in a nation where some believe that culture and race do not matter and others beg to differ? Barack Obama, in his race to become the Democratic nominee for president of the United States, was compelled to give a speech on race in which he embraced his multiple identities. His speech was immediately compared with Dr. Martin Luther King, Jr.'s "I Have a Dream" speech delivered forty-three years earlier. Both texts insist that the destiny of the United States depends on the connectedness of the nation's citizens.

Then there is the question of text and morality. Where has God gone? Biblical texts were central to both African American disenfranchisement (Ephesians 6:5, "Servants, be obedient to them that are your masters," for example) *and* development (the insurrectionist spirit inspired by the blood-and-doom passages of the Old Testament). Gabriel Prosser meditated on the Bible and dreamed of a black state. Denmark Vesey found strength in these words of Joshua: "And they utterly destroyed all that was in the city, both man and ox, and sheep and ass, with the edge of a sword." Nat Turner, too, used the Bible to spark his insurrection. The words "from that time began Jesus to show unto his disciples, that he must go to Jerusalem, and suffer many things of the elders and chief priests and scribes, and be killed" (Matthew 16:21) released him from the fear of death.

Strong, purposeful texts lead men to act in and on their times. They

- Provide inspiration

- Provide spiritual nourishment

- Ignite the struggle for equality

- Nurture awareness of historical events and important persons

- Identify and restore historical continuity

- Lead men and women to demand respect as first-class citizens

Connections among reading, writing, speaking, and action are salient in the history of the literacy development of African American males, from old men on the corner talking shit to literature on guerilla warfare. Ideological texts such as *Listen, Yankee* (Mills 1960) and *The Black Jacobins* (James 1938/1980) offer young black men an intellectual apprenticeship and engender social and political consciousness. Consider these statements:

- I thank God for making me a man (Frederick Douglass)

- I thank God for making me a black man (Martin Delaney)

- If a man hasn't discovered something that he will die for, he isn't fit to live (Dr. Martin Luther King, Jr.)

- If I am not for myself, who is for me? And when I am for myself, what am I? And if not now, when? (Rabbi Hillel)

Engaging African American Adolescent Male Voices

Power and promise do not rest in a prescribed list of texts, but in *identifying* texts. Seeking out these texts, I do a number of things.

1. Think deeply about the role of literacy instruction in relation to today's adolescents

2. Read extensively with African American adolescent males in mind

3. Collaborate with African American adolescent males

4. Engage and listen to their voices

5. Reflect on their engagement/disengagement with text (Figure 8.2 identifies several forces that heighten African American males engagement with text).

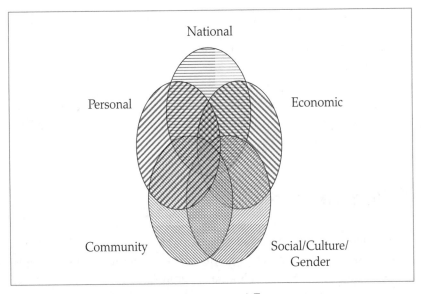

Fig. 8.2: *Forces That Heighten Engagement with Text*

In identifying texts that African American adolescent males find meaningful and significant, we need to make the young male's voices and viewpoints part of the equation. To obtain this information I give students a number of texts to choose from, ask them to read several of them, then use the following questions to elicit their responses:

1. Which texts have been most useful to you?

2. Which texts have been least useful to you?

3. How did the texts affect your reading?

4. How did the texts affect your views of yourself?

5. Which texts would you recommend to other teenage African American males? Why?

6. Which texts would you not recommend to other teenage African American males? Why?

7. How are the texts similar to the texts you read in school?

8. How are the texts different from the texts you read in school?

9. What is most engaging about the texts?

10. What is least engaging about the texts?

11. How are the texts helping you think differently?

12. Do you want to add anything about the texts that I did not ask about?

These text-related discussions provide valuable insights for shaping educational contexts and selecting and mediating text with African American adolescent males who struggle with reading.

So Where's the List?

To reconnect African American adolescent males to text and rebuild their textual lineages, we need to change the way we determine curriculum—a process currently devoid of their input. African American adolescent males should be invited to participate in small, manageable short-term focus groups and literacy collaboratives (seven to ten members) that have been formed to discuss a range of texts: poetry, short stories, essays, speeches, newspaper clippings, and longer fictional and nonfictional pieces.

In addition, identifying characteristics of texts that engage students needs to be part of ongoing assessment wherever possible. Informally, teachers are already assessing how students respond to texts. This needs to become more systematic—that is, planned, recorded, analyzed, and discussed. This is the only way to improve African American adolescent males' relationship with texts.

Nevertheless, we need a starting point. To that end, Appendix B lists texts that African American males have responded to favorably when I've used them in or outside school; Appendix C lists all the texts I've mentioned in this book (there is naturally some overlap). Finally, in Appendix D, I have taken ten of these texts and added both "starters" (excerpts that can be used to introduce the texts to students) and two essential questions that can be used to frame your instruction and discussion. (A caveat here—each instructional context is different, and needs to be considered on its own terms.)

Ultimately, each generation of African American adolescent males will judge for themselves whether to engage or disengage. Because these young men are unique and face their own challenges, they must identify texts that mark *their* times and *their* lives. If we create opportunities for this to happen in schools and other social institutions, they will not only begin to trust the texts, they will begin to trust us too. Then maybe we'll hear one of them say, "Education is on my side" or "I used to keep it gutter, but now I am all good." This is my hope.

Sample Lesson with Explicit Instruction and Text

The instructional focus in this lesson is on monitoring comprehension and responding to think-and-search questions (Raphael and Au 2006). I included a word bank because this was the students' first time completing this type of activity. I used excerpts from the text to teach skills and strategies, in essence *using the text to teach the text.* This approach is effective because it uses repeated readings to nurture reading fluency, a strategy that can be used in all disciplines.

Name _____   ____/6

Complete the following cloze activity. Be sure you insert words that make sense in the place where you insert them.

Look at the example.

My _____ is John

Choice A: My <u>nose</u> is John. (Incorrect; *nose* does not make sense)

Choice B: My <u>name</u> is John. (Correct; *name* makes sense)

Choice C: My <u>friend</u> is John. (Correct; you can have a friend named John)

Choice D: My <u>class</u> is John. (Incorrect; *class* does not make sense)

I did not start off this way. I don't know what happened to me. I am not writing this note for your _____. I think I deserve to die for what I did—I killed. I took a life. The only thing I can _____ in return, that is fair, is my own life. The penalty for taking someone's life is _____ my own life.

All of my fourteen years have come to this point—wasted. I am telling my story because I want you to _____ me. I would rather be riding a bike or learning a new _____, something foreign. I would like to see different parts of the world like Central America or China. I would like to have a Chinese friend. For some reason, I think Chinese kids are cool. They _____ with those funny symbols and eat with chopsticks. I wish I could hear music from a piano roll off my fingertips.

Words to choose from:

offer	sympathy
understand	giving
write	language

Think-and-Search Question: This boy is writing because he wants
   a) to die
   b) to be understood
   c) to have a Chinese friend
   d) to see different parts of the world

Let's read the following text to find out more about the young boy. Pay particular attention to his call for being understood.

Crossfire: A Note from a Drive-By Shooter
by Alfred W. Tatum

I wanted to reach out and grab the bullet the moment I heard the bang. Too late. I am doomed, I thought. I heard the screams. I am now running scared. I tried to convince myself that a killer is not supposed to have feelings. We are supposed to hate, hate everything. Right now, I hate myself. Nobody wants to hear this. I am a killer. I killed someone's son, someone's brother, and someone's nephew. I killed somebody who looks like me. In a way, I killed myself twice.

I did not start off this way. I don't know what happened to me. I am not writing this note for your sympathy. I think I deserve to die for what I did—I killed. I took a life. The only thing I can offer in return, that is fair, is my own life. The penalty for taking someone's life is giving my own life. All of my fourteen years have come to this point—wasted. I am telling my story because I want you to understand me. I would rather be riding a bike or learning a new language, something foreign. I would like to see different parts of the world like Central America or China. I would like to have a Chinese friend. For some reason, I think Chinese kids are cool. They write with those funny symbols and eat with chopsticks. I wish I could hear music from a piano roll off my fingertips.

Please no pity.

Do not start feeling sorry for me.

Too late for that.

Just read the letter and try to understand me.

Letter

April 13, 2006

Dear Reader,

i have two parents who love me. They always bought me new clothes and my favorite gym shoes, New Balance. Although everyone else loved Nikes, i loved New Balances. i had a pair on the day i pulled the trigger. Clean. i always keep them cleaned. i am afraid to think about the blood-soaked stain on the boy i shot. i always kept my stuff clean. And now someone became blood-soaked because of me. i saw the picture on the Internet the next day. He lay there slumped over in a pool of blood because of me. A lady was screaming in the background. The boy's name was Justin. i found out he was younger than me, thirteen.

There is something about a young person being dead that is not right. A kid will be placed in a coffin because of me. As the car i was in drove away, i glanced back and saw his face slam into the concrete. He did not try to catch himself or turn away. His body simply titled forward and picked up speed as it dropped. My body jerked as if i felt the thump of the ground. Bam!

Just yesterday, i was in class looking at a periodic table of elements. i could tell you about all of the earth's precious metals. AU is the symbol on the periodic table used for gold. It has an atomic number of 79. Most of my friends only know that water is called H_2O, but they do not know that it is made up of two atoms of hydrogen and one atom of oxygen, giving it an atomic number of 3. i started learning about the periodic table at a science camp held over the summer at the University of Illinois at Chicago. It was only fifteen minutes away from the west side where i live—the same west side where i killed. i killed somebody over the atomic number 79, a funky gold chain. Gold and iron clashed. The symbol for iron is FE and it has an atomic number of 26. It is called a transition metal. Iron has a silver color, the color of the barrel of the gun.

i know you may be wondering why i am writing with a small i. It is not a mistake. My dad always told me that i have to earn the right to write with a big i. He told me that there is power in a thing when a person earns the right to name himself. i am afraid that i will never be able to name myself. Others will name me. Murderer. Convict. Delinquent. Thug. Monster. None of these feel like they fit me. i used to be called the science boy last year because i love science. I won the science fair last year with a project on the human brain. My grandfather started calling me Brains after that. I remember being called the teacher's pet and momma's boy when i was younger. Murderer, convict, delinquent, thug, or monster does not seem to fit. But, the law of physics tells us that for every action there is a reaction.

1. Why did the killer's body jerk?
   a. He was shot.
   b. He slammed into the ground.
   c. He felt bad because of what happened.

2. Why did the shooter start talking about the periodic table?
   a. To brag about being good in science.
   b. To explain why he murdered someone.
   c. To describe the science camp.

3. Why is the shooter writing with the small i? Do you agree with his decision? Why or why not?

Forty Engaging Texts for African American Adolescent Males

A Letter to African American Males, by Frank W. Hale (nonfiction) (middle school/high school/university)

Appeal to the Coloured Citizens of the World, by David Walker (nonfiction) (middle school/high school/university)

Autobiography of Malcolm X, by Malcolm X and Alex Haley (nonfiction) (middle school/high school)

Bang, by Sharon Flake (novel) (middle school)

Beast of No Nation, by Uzodinma Iweala (novel) (high school)

Black Boy, by Richard Wright (nonfiction) (middle school/high school)

Black Men: Obsolete, Single, or Dangerous, by Haki Madhubuti (nonfiction) (high school/university)

The Call of the Wild, by Jack London (novel) (high school)

Convicted in the Womb: One Man's Journey from Prisoner to Peacemaker, by Carl Upchurch (nonfiction) (high school/university)

Dark Alliance: The CIA, the Contras, and the Crack Cocaine Explosion, by Gary Webb (nonfiction) (high school/university)

"The Declaration of Independence," by Thomas Jefferson (manifesto) (middle school/high school/university)

"The Fiftieth Anniversary of *Brown vs. Board of Education,*" by Bill Cosby (speech) (middle school/high school/university)

The First Part Last, by Angela Johnson (novel) (middle school/high school)

47, by Walter Mosley (novel) (middle school)

Handbook for Boys, by Walter Dean Myers (novel) (middle school/high school)

"If We Must Die," by Claude McKay (poem) (middle school/high school/university)

"Invictus," by William Henley (poem) (middle school/high school/university)

The Killing of Edmund Perry, by Robert Anson (nonfiction) (high school)

Letters to a Young Brother, by Hill Harper (nonfiction) (high school)

"The Masque of Red Death," by Edgar Allan Poe (short story) (high school/university)

Miracle at Monty Middle School, by Mary A. Monroe (novel) (middle school)

Monster: Autobiography of an L.A. Gang Member, by Sanyika Shakur (nonfiction) (university)

My Grandfather's Son: A Memoir, by Clarence Thomas (nonfiction) (high school/university)

Narrative of the Life of Frederick Douglass, by Frederick Douglass (nonfiction) (middle school/high school)

No Turning Back: A Novel of South Africa, by Beverly Naidoo (novel) (middle school)

Our America: Life and Death on the South Side of Chicago, by LeAlan Jones and Lloyd Newman (nonfiction) (high school)

The Pact, by Sampson Davis, George Jenkins, and Rameck Hunt (nonfiction) (high school/university)

A Personal Odyssey, by Thomas Sowell (nonfiction) (high school/university)

The Piano Lesson, by August Wilson (play) (high school/university)

Public Enemy #2, by Aaron McGruder (comic book) (middle school/high school)

A Raisin in the Sun, by Lorraine Hansberry (play) (high school/university)

Reallionaire, by Farah Gray (nonfiction) (middle school/high school)

"The Revolt of the Evil Fairies," by Ted Posten (short story) (middle school)

A Right to Be Hostile, by Aaron McGruder (comic book) (middle school/high school)

"Self-Reliance," by Ralph Waldo Emerson (essay) (high school/university)

"Test of a Man," by Anonymous (poem) (middle school/high school/university)

Up from Slavery, by Booker T. Washington (nonfiction) (middle school/high school)

We Beat the Street, by Sampson Davis, George Jenkins, and Rameck Hunt (nonfiction) (middle school/high school)

Yo' Little Brother, by Anthony Davis and Jeffrey Jackson (nonfiction) (middle school/high school)

You Hear Me? Poems and Writing by Teenage Boys, by Betsy Franco (anthology) (high school)

Texts Mentioned in This Book

Teachers frequently ask me for suggestions for books to suggest to the young males in their classes. Below are the titles I've mentioned in this book. However, some of these are not developmentally appropriate for adolescent readers.

Almos' a Man
The Almost White Boy
America
Appeal to the Coloured Citizens of the World
Are You There God? It's Me, Margaret
Authentically Black
Autobiography of an L.A. Gang Member
Autobiography of Malcolm X
Bang
Be Boy Buzz
Before the Mayflower
Beloved
Best Short Stories by Black Writers 1899–1967
The Bible
Black Art
Black Boy
Black Jacobians
Black Skin, White Masks
Blindness
Blood in My Eye
Blue Back Speller
Bronx Masquerade

Bronzeville Boys and Girls
Classic Slave Narratives
The Color of Water: A Black Man's Guide to His White Mother
Columbian Orator
Convicted in the Womb
"The Declaration of Independence"
Die Nigger Die!
Discover the Power Within You
The Fire Next Time
The First Part Last
Forged by Fire
Gifted Hands
Guerilla Warfare
"I Have a Dream"
"If We Must Die"
"Invictus"
Invisible Man
Kaffir Boy
Das Kapital
The Learning Tree
Leaves of Grass
The Liberator
Lift Every Voice and Sing
Listen, Yankee
Locomotion
Lynching for Profit
Marijuana and a Pistol
Message to the Blackman in America
The Miseducation of the Negro
Mother to Son
Narrative of the Life of Frederick Douglass
Native Son
Negroes with Guns
Nigger
Night
145th Street: Short Stories
Pass It On
Pursuit of Happyness
Quitting America

A Raisin in the Sun

Reallionaire

The Rebel

Red Scarf Girl: A Memoir of the Cultural Revolution

"The Revolt of the Evil Fairies"

Seven Storey Mountain

Shame of a Nation

Sixteen Ways to Look at a Black Man

Soledad Brothers: The Prison Letters of George Jackson

Soul on Ice

The Souls of Black Folk

Sounder

SOS

The State and the Revolution

Stolen Legacy

Sula

Tally's Corner

"Test of a Man"

They Came Before Columbus

Think Big

To Be a Slave

Two Thousand Seasons

Uncle Tom's Cabin

Up from Slavery

Vintage Hughes

Visions for Black Men

We Wear the Mask

What Should I Do Without Him

Why We Can't Wait

Wings

Winning the Race

Wretched of the Earth

Youth

Ten Enabling Texts with Starters and Essential Questions

TEXT	STARTERS	ESSENTIAL QUESTIONS
47, by Walter Mosley	And every night they chained your feet to an eyebolt in the floor. The men out there were mostly angry and so they were always fighting or crying of just plain sad. (12)	What are the alternatives when someone tries to stamp out the existence of others? Are there appropriate responses? Inappropriate responses?
Bang, by Sharon Flake	A black boy don't get a hundred chances to get it right. Sometimes he just gets one. That's it. . . . You blow your chance, you blow your life. (124)	Is the United States a redemptive society? Is the society constructed to save some and sacrifice others?
Enough, by Juan Williams	Dr. King said he wanted to get black people to shed the idea that they did not control their destiny, an idea he attributed to the power of racists to infect black people with self-defeating doubts about inferiority and create a psychological need to rely on whites for their well-being. (40)	Is victim mentality real or imagined? Who has greater authority over an individual's destiny—the inner enemy or the outer enemy?

continues

TEXT	STARTERS	ESSENTIAL QUESTIONS
Handbook for Boys, by Walter Dean Myers	The problem with so many young men . . . is that when they're young, they really don't know how to get their lives together. . . . After a while they just give up and start talking about how they really don't care. (135)	How does one recover a part of one's soul? What does it take to escape vulnerability-producing conditions unscathed?
Monster: The Autobiography of an L.A. Gang Member, by Sanyika Shakur	The following quote by Malcolm X impressed the author: Out of frustration and hopelessness our young people have reached the point of no return. We no longer endorse patience or turning the other cheek. (214)	How does a person become reconciled to a different identity? Does a person become a "monster" by choice or are they forced into becoming a "monster"?
My Grandfather's Son: A Memoir, by Clarence Thomas	Our small, soft hands blistered quickly at the start of each summer, but Daddy never let us wear work gloves, which he considered a sign of weakness. After a few weeks of constant work, the bloody blisters gave way to hard-earned calluses that protected us from pain. Long after the fact, it occurred to me that this was a metaphor for life—blisters come before calluses, vulnerability before maturity. (25)	What are you willing to sacrifice to create the life you want to live? What do you need to know in order to endure polarizing differences?
Narrative of the Life of Frederick Douglass, by Frederick Douglass	I often found myself regretting my own existence. (55)	What does it mean to exist? What are the factors that contribute to one's existence?

TEXT	STARTERS	ESSENTIAL QUESTIONS
"Self-Reliance," by Ralph Waldo Emerson (essay)	Whoso would be a man must be a non-conformist.	Is there more value in conformity or nonconformity? Can individuals be truly self-reliant in our society today?
The Envy of the World: On Being a Black Man in America, by Ellis Cose	We tend to react in one of two ways: We either embrace the role we are told constantly that we are expected to play, or we reject the script and endeavor to create our own. (3) Black men are not an "endangered species". . . . We stand nearly seventeen million strong, an ever-growing extended family of black boys and men. (17)	In a global society, does the collective identity of individual groups matter? Is it more important to be group-identified or viewed as part of the human fabric?
The First Part Last, by Angela Johnson (the words *fuck* and *shit* appear in the text)	The only way to change something is to pay attention to the signs. (51)	During difficult times, is it better to rely on the facts or to rely on faith? Which is the better teacher—success or failure?

Study Guide Questions

Introduction:

On page 12, Tatum writes that as he "thinks about the literacy development of African American adolescent males" he is challenged by a series of questions. Choose two or three of them, listed below, to discuss with your group.

1. How are we conceptualizing literacy instruction for them?

2. How are we teaching these boys how to read and write and what texts are we using?

3. How do policies, mandates, curricula, and personal beliefs affect teachers who are genuinely concerned with addressing the literacy needs of these young men?

4. How are we nurturing the *identities* of these young males?

5. How are we supporting these young males to believe in themselves as academic, cultural, economic, human, social, and spiritual beings?

6. How are we helping these young males enjoy school?

Chapter 1:

Chapter 1 begins with an essential question for students and educators: How do I become and remain resilient? Discuss what this means in your personal and professional life. As a follow-up, discuss how you might help your students become (and remain) resilient.

Chapter 2:

◆ Bring to your study group a list of the texts you currently assign to your students. All together, ask yourselves the provocative questions Tatum poses on page 28.

  ◆ Out of all the texts in the world, why do we want to put these texts in front of African American adolescent males living in high-poverty communities?

  ◆ If I only had three to five texts to use with my students, which texts would I use?

Chapter 3:

In this chapter, Tatum discusses what he calls the "Vital Signs of Literacy Instruction" and four parallel gaps that may occur if these vital signs are not addressed.

◆ A reading achievement gap

◆ A relationship gap

◆ A rigor gap

◆ A responsiveness gap

Reexamine the table on page 45 where he lays out the vital signs and corresponding gaps, and discuss these questions and topics.

◆ How do you think you are doing in addressing students' needs in each area? In your classroom? In your school? Are there gaps?

◆ If there are gaps, work together to create a list of actions you might take individually or collectively to address and close the gaps.

Chapter 4:

Tatum used the texts in Figure 4.3 (page 79) "to identify the [four] characteristics of texts that African American males found significant and meaningful."

1. They provided a healthy psyche

2. They provided modern awareness of the real world

3. They focused on the collective struggle of African Americans

4. They served as a road map for being, doing, thinking, and acting

    ◆ Bring to your group a text that you currently assign or are considering assigning to your students. Together, try what Tatum asks at the chapter's end: "Audit [the] texts for enabling characteristics for African American adolescent males anchored by a clear definition for the role of literacy development for these young men."

    ◆ Together, try to identify texts that may be a radical departure from what is being offered to economically disadvantaged African American adolescent males attending today's middle and high schools and other social and educational institutions. Come up with a short list that you are willing to try in your own classrooms.

Chapter 5:

◆ Use the framework for mediating text (see Figures 5.2 and 5.3, pages 92–94) with a short literary or nonliterary selection that you believe is an enabling text for your students. Avoid co-opting the text with the framework. Ultimately, it's the texts that matter, particularly if the selection of the texts is guided by something deeply purposeful.

◆ After you teach the text, gauge the students' views about the lessons. Reflect together and discuss your classroom experiences with the lesson. Use students' response to your lesson to plan subsequent lessons.

◆ Draft your own textual lineage and bring it to your study group. Provide rationales for the texts in your lineage and share why they had an impact on you. (See Figure 8.1, "My Middle and High School Textual Lineage," at the beginning of Chapter 8 [page 132] for an example.)

Chapter 6:

Have each member of your group choose a poetic broadside to share with their students. Discuss your choices together—why you think it is an enabling text, and so on. After you each use the poem you chose in your classrooms, discuss how the lessons went. What worked and what did not? How might you revise the lesson—or move forward from here?

Chapter 7:

Have each member of your group choose a "black short" to share with their students. Discuss your choices together. After you each use the short story you chose in your classrooms, discuss how the lessons went. What worked and what did not? How might you revise the lesson—or move forward from here?

Chapter 8:

In this chapter, Tatum writes that "the examination of the characteristics of texts that engage students needs to be a part of the ongoing assessment process in schools. . . . Informally, teachers are already assessing how students respond to texts. This needs to become more systematic . . . planned, recorded, analyzed, and discussed. This is the only way to truly record African American adolescent males' relationship with text."

On page 138, Tatum shares his interview protocol that he uses with students to assess the "approximate types of texts that engage them." Then he writes:

> Curricula selection is now devoid of adolescents' input. African American adolescent males should be invited to participate in short-term focus groups and short-term case studies. A range of texts that include poetry, short stories, essays, speeches, newspaper clippings, and longer fictional and non-fictional pieces should be selected for the focus groups and case studies. Time should be set aside to discuss texts with African American males in literacy collaboratives. The groups should be small and manageable, roughly seven to ten African American male students.

Work together as a group, or individually, to set up short-term focus groups with African American male students. Select and provide students with several texts in advance. If you'd like, use Tatum's interview protocol with students. Come back together with your study group and discuss your experience, how it impacted your thinking, and how you might move forward from here.

Bibliography

Akbar, N. 1991. *Visions for Black Men.* Tallahassee, FL: Mind Productions.

Anson, R. 1987. *Best Intentions: The Education and Killing of Edmund Perry.* New York: Vintage.

Armah, A. K. 1973/2000. *Two Thousand Seasons.* Popenguine, Senegal: Per Ankh.

Asante, M. 2003. *Erasing Racism.* Amherst, NY: Prometheus Books.

Baldwin, J. 1953. *Go Tell It on the Mountain.* New York: Laurel.

———. 1963. *The Fire Next Time.* New York: Dial Press.

Beach, R., D. Appleman, S. Hynds, and J. Wilhelm. 2006. *Teaching Literature to Adolescents.* Mahwah, NJ: Lawrence Erlbaum.

Belt-Beyan, P. 2004. *The Emergence of African American Literacy Traditions.* Westport, CT: Praeger.

Bennett, L. 1982. *Before the Mayflower.* New York: Penguin Books.

Bernstein, N. 2005. *All Alone in the World: Children of the Incarcerated.* New York: New Press.

Blight, D., ed. 1998. *The Columbian Orator.* New York: New York University Press.

Blume, J. 1970. *Are You There God? It's Me, Margaret.* New York: Bantam.

Brown, H. R. 1969/2002. *Die Nigger Die.* Chicago, IL: Lawrence Hill Books.

Butterworth, E. 1992. *Discover the Power Within You.* New York: HarperCollins.

Camus, A. 1956. *The Rebel.* New York: Alfred Knopf.

Carmichael, S. 2003. *Ready for Revolution: The Life and Struggles of Stokely Carmichael.* New York: Scribner.

Carson, B. 1990. *Gifted Hands: The Ben Carson Story.* Grand Rapids, MI: Zondervan.

————. 1992. *Think Big: Unleashing Your Potential for Excellence.* New York: Harper.

Cleaver, E. 1968. *Soul on Ice.* New York: Delta.

Coetzee, J. M. 2002. *Youth: Scenes from Provincial Life II.* New York: Penguin.

Collins, P. 2006. *From Black Power to Hip Hop: Racism, Nationalism, and Feminism.* Philadelphia, PA: Temple University Press.

Coombs, O. 1971. *What We Must See: Young Black Storytellers.* New York: Dodd, Mead & Company.

Cosby, W. 2004. Address at the NAACP's Commemoration of the Fiftieth Anniversary of *Brown v. Board of Education.* http://www.americanrhetoric .com/speeches/billcosbypoundcakespeech.htm (accessed December 7, 2007).

Cose, E. 2002. *The Envy of the World: On Being a Black Man in America.* New York: Washington Square Press.

Davis, A., and J. Jackson. 1998. *Yo', Little Brother.* Chicago: African American Images.

Douglass, F. 1845/1997. *Narrative of the Life of Frederick Douglass, an American Slave.* New York: Signet Classics.

Draper, S. 1997. *Forged by Fire.* New York: Simon Pulse.

Du Bois, W. E. B. 1903. *The Souls of Black Folk.* New York: Signet.

————. 2001. *The Education of Black People: Ten Critiques, 1906–1960.* New York: Monthly Review Press.

Dyson, M. 2004. *The Michael Eric Dyson Reader.* New York: Basic Civitas Books.

Ellison, R. 1947. *Invisible Man.* New York: Random House.

Fanon, F. 1963. *The Wretched of the Earth.* New York: Grove Press.

————. 1967. *Black Skin, White Masks.* New York: Grove Press.

Flake, S. 2005. *Bang.* New York: Hyperion.

Foner, P. 1970. *The Black Panthers Speak.* Cambridge, MA: Da Capo Press.

Gable, C. 2004. *Ebony Rising: Short Fiction of the Greater Harlem Renaissance Era.* Bloomington, IN: Indiana University Press.

Gardner, C. 2006. *The Pursuit of Happyness.* New York: Amistad.

Gardner, H. 2006. *Changing Minds: The Art and Science of Changing Our Own and Other People's Minds.* Boston, MA: Harvard Business School Press.

Garrison, W. 1831. "Inaugural Editorial." *The Liberator,* January 7, 1831.

Gates, H. L. 2004. *America Behind the Color Line.* New York: Warner Books.

Gay, G. 2000. *Culturally Responsive Teaching: Theory, Research, and Practice.* New York: Teachers College Press.

Goodenow, C. 1993. Classroom "Belonging Among Early Adolescent Students: Relationships to Motivation and Achievement." *Journal of Early Adolescence* 13: 21–43.

Goodman, J. 1994. *Stories of Scottsboro.* New York: Vintage.

Gray, F. 2004. *Reallionaire: Nine Steps to Becoming Rich from the Inside Out.* Deerfield Beach, FL: Health Communications.

Gregory, D. 1964. *Nigger.* New York: Pocket Books.

Greenlee, S. 1969/2002. *The Spook Who Sat by the Door.* Chicago, IL: Lushena Books.

Grimes, N. 2002. *Bronx Masquerade.* New York: Speak.

Guevara, C. 1961. *Guerilla Warfare.* New York: Monthly Review Press.

Haley, A., and Malcolm X. 1965. *The Autobiography of Malcolm X.* New York: Ballantine Books.

Hansberry, L. 1959. *A Raisin in the Sun.* New York: Vintage.

Hogue, W. L. 2003. *The African American Male, Writing, and Difference.* New York: State University of New York Press.

Hooper, L. 2007. *The Art of Work: The Art and Life of Haki Madhubuti.* Chicago, IL: Third World Press.

Hughes, L. (Ed.) 1967. *The Best Short Stories by Black Writers, 1899–1967: The Classic Anthology.* Boston, MA: Little Brown and Company.

Iweala, U. 2007. *Beasts of No Nation.* New York: HarperCollins.

Jackson, G. 1970. *Soledad Brother: The Prison Letters of George Jackson.* New York: Coward-McCann.

———. 1972/1990. *Blood in My Eye.* Baltimore, MD: Black Classic Press.

James, C. L. R. 1938/1980. *The Black Jacobins.* 3rd ed. London: Allison and Busby.

James, G. 1954. *Stolen Legacy: Greek Philosophy Is Stolen Egyptian Philosophy.* Trenton, NJ: Africa World Press.

Jiang, J. 1997. *Red Scarf Girl: A Memoir of the Cultural Revolution.* New York: HarperTrophy.

Johnson, A. 2003. *The First Part Last.* New York: Simon Pulse.

Johnson, C., and P. Smith. 1998. *Africans in America: America's Journey Through Slavery.* New York: Harcourt.

Johnson, J. W. 1927. *God's Trombones: Seven Negro Sermons in Verse.* New York: Viking Press.

Kakutani, M. 2009. "From Books, New President Found Voice." *The New York Times,* January 19.

King, M. L. 1963. *Why We Can't Wait.* New York: Harper & Row.

King, W. 1972. *Black Short Story Anthology.* New York: Columbia University Press.

Kotlowitz, A. 1991. *There Are No Children Here: The Story of Two Boys Growing Up in the Other America.* New York: Anchor Books.

Kozol, J. 2005. *The Shame of the Nation: The Restoration of Apartheid Schooling in America.* New York: Crown Publishers.

Lareau, A. 2003. *Unequal Childhoods: Class, Race, and Family Life.* Berkeley, CA: University of California Press.

Lenin, V. I. 1918/1992. *The State and Revolution.* New York: Penguin Books.

Lester, J. 1998. *To Be a Slave.* New York: Puffin.

Liebow, E. 1967. *Tally's Corner: A Study of Negro Streetcorner Men.* Boston, MA: Little, Brown and Company.

Lilien, J. 2001. MHC Lectures Traces Literary Circle History. http:// media.www. dailycollegian.com/media/storage/paper874/news/2001/10/12/News/Mhc-Lectures.Traces.Literary.Circle.History-1549192.shtml (accessed December 29, 2008).

Manza, J., and C. Uggen. 2006. *Locked Out: Felon Disenfranchisement and American Democracy.* New York: Oxford University Press.

Mason, C. 2004. *The African-American Bookshelf: Fifty Must-Reads from Before the Civil War Through Today.* New York: Citadel Press.

Mathabane, M. 1986. *Kaffir Boy: The True Story of a Black Youth's Coming of Age in Apartheid South Africa.* New York: Plume.

McBride, J. 1996. *The Color of Water: A Black Man's Tribute to His White Mother.* New York: Riverhead Books.

McWhorter, J. 2003. *Authentically Black.* New York: Gotham Books.

McWhorter, J. 2006. *Winning the Race: Beyond the Crisis in Black America.* New York: Gotham Books.

Merton, T. 1948. *The Seven Storey Mountain: An Autobiography of Faith.* Orlando, FL: Harcourt Brace.

Miller, D. 1988. *Frederick Douglass and the Fight for Freedom.* New York: Facts on-File Publication.

Mills, C. W. 1956. *The Power Elite.* New York: Oxford University Press.

———. 1960. *Listen Yankee: The Revolution in Cuba.* New York: Ballantine Books.

Morrison, T. 1987. *Beloved.* New York: Knopf.

———. 2004. *Sula.* New York: Vintage International.

Muhammad, E. 1965. *Message to the Blackman in America.* Maryland Height, MO: Secretarius Memps.

Murtadha-Watts, K. 2000. "Theorizing Urban Black Masculinity Construction in an African-Centered School." In *Masculinities at School,* ed. N. Lesko. Thousand Oaks, CA: Sage Publications.

Myers, W. D. 1995. *The Glory Field.* New York: Scholastic.

———. 2002. *Handbook for Boys: A Novel.* New York: HarperTrophy.

———. 2003. *The Beast.* New York: Scholastic.

Naidoo, B. 1995. *No Turning Back: A Novel of South Africa.* New York: HarperTrophy.

Naylor, G. 1995. *Children of the Night: The Best Short Stories by Black Writers, 1967 to the Present.* Boston, MA: Little, Brown and Company.

Parks, G. 1963. *Born Black.* Philadelphia, PA: J. B. Lippincott.

———. 1963. *The Learning Tree.* New York: Ballantine Books.

Perry, I. 2004. *Prophets of the Hood: Politics and Poetics in Hip Hop.* Durham, NC: Duke University Press.

Price, J. 2000. "Peer (Dis)connections, School, and African American Masculinities." In *Masculinities at School,* ed. N. Lesko. Thousand Oaks, CA: Sage Publications.

Raphael, T. E., and K. H. Au. 2006. *QAR Now: Question Answer Relationships.* New York: Scholastic.

Reid, M. 2002. *Black Protest Poetry: Polemics from the Harlem Renaissance and the Sixties.* New York: Peter Lang Publishers.

Robinson, R. 2004. *Quitting America.* New York: Dutton.

Roessel, R., and A. Rampersand. 2006. *Langston Hughes: Poetry for Young People.* New York: Sterling.

Saramago, J. 1997. *Blindness.* Orlando, FL: Harcourt.

Schmidt, P. and W. Ma. 2006. *50 Literacy Strategies for Culturally Responsive Teaching, K–8.* Thousand Oaks, CA: Corwin Press.

Shakur, S. 1993. *Monster: The Autobiography of an L.A. Gang Member.* New York: Penguin.

Smith, M., and J. Wilhelm. 2006. *Going with the Flow: How to Engage Boys (and Girls) in Their Literacy Learning.* Portsmouth, NH: Heinemann.

Sowell, T. 2000. *A Personal Odyssey.* New York: Touchstone.

Spencer, M. B. 1999. "Social and Cultural Influences on School Adjustment: The Application of an Identity-Focused Cultural Ecological Perspective." *Educational Psychologist* 34(1): 43–57.

Stowe, H. B. 1852/2002. *Uncle Tom's Cabin or, Life Among the Lowly.* New York: Aladdin Classics.

Suskind, R. 1999. *A Hope in the Unseen: An American Odyssey from the Inner City to the Ivy League.* New York: Random House.

Tatum, A. W. 2000. "Breaking Down Barriers That Disenfranchise African American Adolescents in Low-Level Reading Tracks." *Journal of Adolescent & Adult Literacy* 44: 52–64.

———. 2002. "Professional Development for Teachers of African American Adolescents." *Illinois Reading Council Journal* 30(1): 42–52.

———. 2003. Advancing the Literacies of African American Adolescents: A Case Study of Professional Development. Unpublished PhD diss., University of Illinois at Chicago.

———. 2005. *Teaching Reading to Black Adolescent Males: Closing the Achievement Gap.* Portsmouth, ME: Stenhouse.

———. 2006a. "Engaging African American Males in Reading." *Educational Leadership* 63(5): 44–49.

———. 2006b. Adolescent Multiple Identities and Teacher Professional Development. In *Reconceptualizing the Literacies in Adolescents' Lives*, eds. D. Alvermann, K. Hinchman, D. Moore, S. Phelps, and D. Waff, 65–79. Mahwah, NJ: Erlbaum.

———. 2008. "Toward a More Anatomically Complete Model of Literacy Instruction: A Focus on African American Male Adolescents and Texts." *Harvard Educational Review* 78(1): 155–180.

———. unpublished. *Chip Chop: A Novel for Black Boys.*

Thomas, C. 2007. *My Grandfather's Son: A Memoir.*

Trotsky, L. 1937/1991. *The Revolution Betrayed: What Is the Soviet Union and Where Is It Going?* Detroit, MI: Labor Publications.

Tse-tung, M. 1961/2000. *On Guerilla Warfare.* Champaign, IL: University of Illinois Press.

Upchurch, Carl. 1996. *Convicted in the Womb: One Man's Journey from Prisoner to Peacemaker.* New York: Bantam Books.

U.S. Department of Education, Institute of Education Sciences, National Center for Education Statistics. 2007. *National Assessment of Educational Progress, Reading Assessment.*

Van Deburg, W. 1992. *New Day in Babylon: The Black Power Movement and American Culture, 1965–1975.* Chicago, IL: University of Chicago Press.

Van Sertima, I. 1976. *They Came Before Columbus: The African Presence in Ancient America.* New York: Random House.

Walker, D. 1829–1830/1965. *Appeal: To The Coloured Citizens of the World, but in Particular, and Very Expressly, to Those of the United States of America.* New York: Hill and Wang.

Walter, M. P. 1999. *Suitcase.* New York: Amistad.

Washington, B. T. 1901. *Up from Slavery.* New York: Doubleday.

Watkins, S. C. 2005. *Hip Hop Matters.* Boston, MA: Beacon.

Weatherby, W. J. 1977. *Squaring Off: Mailer vs. Baldwin.* New York: Mason/Charter.

Webster, N. 1824/2002. *The Original Blue Back Speller.* New York: Patriotic Textbook Series.

Wesley, C. H. 1939. "The Negroes of New York in the Emancipation Movement." *Journal of Negro History* 24(1): 65–103.

Whitman, W. 1855/2004. *Leaves of Grass: First and "Death-Bed" Editions.* New York: Barnes & Noble Classics.

Wiesel, E. 1958. *Night.* New York: Hill and Wang.

Williams, H. A. 2005. *Self-Taught: African American Education in Slavery and Freedom.* Chapel Hill, NC: University of North Carolina Press.

Williams, J. 2006. *Enough.* New York: Crown Publishers.

Williams, R. 1998. *Negroes with Guns.* Detroit, MI: Wayne State University Press.

Wilson, W. 1996. *When Work Disappears: The World of the New Urban Poor.* New York: Vintage.

Woodson, C. G. 1933. *The Mis-Education of the Negro.* Washington, DC: Associated Publishers.

Wright, R. 1940. *Native Son.* New York: Harper and Brothers.

———. 1945. *Black Boy: A Record of Childhood and Youth.* New York: Harper-Perennial.

Index